Change for Good:
Making Your Business Sustainable Through a Value-Driven Strategy

By Mary K. Krajci

QUEENSGATE
PRESS

ISBN 978-0-9889262-0-2

Acknowledgments

This book was inspired when I gave a presentation about my consulting work to my friends in Flourish, a women's mentoring group in my hometown. I am enormously grateful to Sheila Bridgland, Elaine Carroll, Deb Green, Deb Kennedy and Elizabeth Rose for their wise counsel and encouragement. Their friendship and support has been invaluable to me, both as an author and as a business owner.

I owe a special debt of gratitude to Ned Montgomery and Michael Thomson, who believed in me at a time when placing a woman in a leadership role was a rarity. Leading a diverse group of stakeholders in those early days laid the foundation for all the years that followed. Other mentors who have helped shape my consulting career since then include Sarene Byrne, Loretta D'Agnolo, and Bruce Wallach. I have learned so much from each of them, not just about consulting and business but also about life. Likewise, I have gained so much from the consulting colleagues with whom I have worked over the years, especially Raph Blumkin, Lesley Steer, Laarni Atienza, Yves Salama, Ed Boswell and all the wonderful people at Forum. I have grown in knowledge and understanding with every client engagement, especially those where we were blazing new trails together. A special thanks goes to Susan Bohn, Steve McIntosh, Stacey Panagakis and Matt Kaplan for their willingness to try something new and for placing their trust in me.

My deepest thanks belongs to my family—my beloved parents for their lifelong encouragement and inspiration, and my siblings Cin and Jeff for their unflagging support. I dedicate this book to them.

Graphic elements herein adapted from
Microsoft Visio and Microsoft ClipArt

Foreword

For decades business managers have made shareholder value and short term profits their top priority, often because they believe that maximizing today's financial performance is the only way to ensure success for themselves and their organizations. This book is based on the premise that, while financial results are important, there are other forms of business capital that are just as vital for long term success, and that business capital comes from how each of us treats our own stakeholders. Our underlying philosophy acknowledges that, one way or another, we're all in this together. By changing our focus to encompass all of our stakeholders, we increase our chances for long term success.

The planning process described in this book includes twelve exercises, many of which will be familiar to our readers and several that are probably new to most of you. Feel free to use and adapt these exercises and incorporate your own terminology and methods to suit your own organization's strategic planning. Individual exercises may be done in isolation or as part of an end-to-end planning process, with subsequent iterations as you respond to new insights and circumstances. They may be combined with other strategic planning exercises not discussed in this book, such as scenario planning, market assessment and competitive analysis, to name a few. The appropriate scope and degree of rigor is unique to each organization and its circumstances; only you can decide what is right for your own organization.

Author's Note

The approach outlined in this book is very much a work in progress. The ideas expressed herein have been developed over the last twenty years, through consulting engagements with many different clients, and I expect these ideas to continue to evolve with every new assignment. The concepts and suggestions are not carved in stone, but rather provide a starting point for further adaptation. I welcome your constructive comments and any ideas you may have to improve the model. I encourage readers to visit our website (www.queensbridgeconsultancy.com) for further information and sharing of ideas.

Contents

Introduction

Sustainability

Sustainability: the capacity to endure; living within the carrying capacity of supporting eco-systems[1]

Few would deny the importance of creating a sustainable future, whether narrowly confined to their own personal lives, their families and their businesses or expanded to include the rest of the world and future generations. It is the natural instinct of every organism, and likewise every organization, to survive long enough to fulfill its purpose and to pass on its genes or leave a lasting legacy for those that follow.

The fundamental premise of this book is that the best way to create such a future for your own organization and the world is by pursuing a value-driven strategy, one that is grounded in a set of core principles that respect and respond to the legitimate concerns of every stakeholder.

What is a stakeholder?

A stakeholder is anyone (or anything, in the case of Planet Earth) who influences, or is affected by, the affairs of an organization. Customers, employees and investors are the most obvious examples, but there are many others, ranging from suppliers and distributors to the media and on-line bloggers and tweeters.

At any given time some stakeholders take an active interest in your business—industry watchdogs and regulators, for example—while others play a more passive role, such as outside industry groups and the environment. Some stakeholders—for instance, buyers and key suppliers—may wield considerable power, while others have more limited influence—minor vendors and local taxpayers, perhaps. Some, such as distributors and trade associations, are *enablers*, helping your organization succeed; others, such as labor unions and regulators, may present potential *barriers* that can impede your progress unless you can find a way to address their concerns.

Your stakeholders and the roles they play are unique to your organization, and they are apt to change over time. For instance, a powerful stakeholder with a strong interest in your business may become less influential in the future (as has happened with labor unions in much of the U.S. private sector and, more recently, the public sector). Alternatively, a peripheral player today may become more influential in the future—a small supplier who develops a breakthrough technology, for example. Special interest groups and local communities may take a sudden interest in your organization's affairs when you launch a new venture or set up business in a new location. A change in the political party in power may cause a corresponding shift in the degree of industry regulation. All of these changes will have an impact, good or bad, on your business.

---

[1] Definition adapted from Wikipedia.com; a more traditional and broader definition than current popular usage of the term

Value-driven: a way of doing business

It behooves your organization to understand your stakeholders and their wants, needs and expectations, now and in the future, and to find a way to provide each stakeholder with value. To remain competitive, you must do so in a unique and compelling way; at the same time, to remain viable, you must receive fair value in exchange. Value is essentially a two-way street; to ensure a sustainable future, both parties must derive value from the relationship.

Value, as we use the term here, is not measured solely in terms of money, time or other quantifiable metrics; value comprises a wide range of qualitative outcomes as well, such as personal enjoyment, job satisfaction, good health, financial security, positive image, and a sense of well-being. It is the exchange of value, both quantitative and qualitative, over time that defines the relationship.

Your organization's value-driven strategy defines how you will create unique value for each of your key stakeholders, and how you will derive value from your relationship with each of them. *Value-driven* has a second, equally important meaning as well. It also defines the core values or principles—such as integrity, transparency, and fairness—that underlie your organization's way of doing business and foster trust between your organization and your stakeholders. We will discuss further the organizational values that drive strategy in Exercise 5.

Framework

This introduction presents a simple framework for developing and implementing a value-driven strategy, comprising the following:

- Three hallmarks of a successful strategy
- Three basic planning steps
- Five categories encompassing the key strategic elements that must be addressed

The remaining chapters describe the planning process in more detail, with sample methods and tools for performing each step.

The Three Hallmarks of a Successful Strategy

There are three hallmarks of a successful value-driven strategy. Each of these hallmarks is essential to achieving the desired outcomes on behalf of your stakeholders.

Clear Focus
Without clarity and a cohesive strategy, efforts can be misdirected and stakeholders left dissatisfied.

Full Integration
Unless the whole organization is aligned and capable of executing, even the best strategy is likely to fail.

Dynamic Process
Because we know that stakeholders' needs and expectations continuously change, staying in tune with those changes is essential.

Clear Focus

The first hallmark looks at the "who, what, and why" of your strategy. *Who are your stakeholders now, and who should they be? What do they expect from you (and from your competitors)? How do they differ from one another, and how are they the same? What else could you provide them that no one currently does? What could you eliminate? What do you need or want from others, and what can you offer in return?*

Recognizing the differences among stakeholders—their relationship over time with your organization, the way they make decisions, the fit between your capabilities and requirements and their needs and concerns—enables you to identify and target key stakeholders and address their needs directly.

Understanding the spoken and hidden needs, the dissatisfiers and delighters, the must-haves and the nice-to-haves, the expectations and perceptions of your stakeholders enables you to develop targeted strategies, provide unique value and deliver the desired outcomes.

Full Integration

The second hallmark addresses the "how, when, and where" of your strategy. *Are the necessary systems, structures and processes in place to support and execute the strategy? Are people capable and committed? Does management actively support the strategy? Have the barriers been eliminated? What are the pitfalls to watch out for?*

The most common reason strategies fail is the inability of the organization to execute, even when the new direction is clear and has been communicated to all levels of the organization. Resources are often misallocated; there is no accountability; the criteria for decision-making are unclear or in conflict; systems and procedures are unduly cumbersome and outdated; people may lack the skills and knowledge to perform. Identifying and correcting these problems is vital to your organization's success.

Dynamic Process

The third and final hallmark is the most often overlooked and hence offers the greatest potential for distinguishing your organization from the rest. Essential to long-run sustainability, it repeatedly and proactively asks the vital questions, *"How are we doing? What's happening?"* As the pace of change continues to accelerate, the ability of your organization to anticipate, identify and adapt to new threats and opportunities in the marketplace is increasingly crucial to survival.

Three Basic Planning Steps

There are three simple, interlocking steps to creating and executing a successful strategy. Each step answers one of three fundamental questions:

Where are we now?
Where do we want to go?
How will we get there?

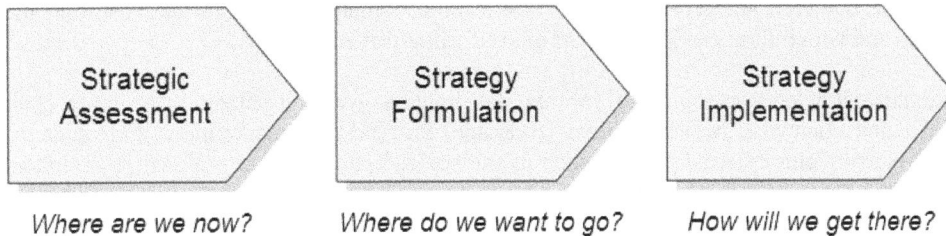

Strategic Assessment	Strategy Formulation	Strategy Implementation
Where are we now?	*Where do we want to go?*	*How will we get there?*

Strategic Assessment

The first planning step answers the fundamental question: *Where are we now?* Taking stock of your organization's history and current circumstances is vital to knowing how to move forward. Knowing your stakeholders and recognizing the relative capabilities of your organization and your competitors—both strengths and weaknesses—enable you to close any gaps between their expectations and your ability to meet them. Assessing the existing and potential opportunities and threats that your organization faces further enables you to anticipate and prepare to meet the challenges of an ever-changing landscape.

Part I addresses Strategic Assessment in further detail.

Strategy Formulation

The second planning step answers the fundamental question: *Where do we want to go?* Once you have a solid understanding of where you are now and what challenges and opportunities you face, you have choices to make about where you ultimately want to be and when you want to get there. The destination and timeframe you choose determine the direction and distance you must travel, and at what pace. Will you stay the course you are on, or will you change direction? Is the destination easily reached, or do you face a long, arduous journey? How will you know you've arrived?

These are the questions you must ask as you set your sights on the future. Part II addresses Strategy Formulation in further detail.

Strategy Implementation

The third and final planning step answers the fundamental question: *How will we get there?* Once you know where you are and where you want to go, the final step is to chart the course and to make the necessary preparations. Who needs to be on board? How will you navigate the inevitable bumps and turns you encounter along the way? How will you track your progress, and how will you know when to adjust your course?

Part III addresses Strategy Implementation in further detail.

Key Strategic Elements

Your organization's strategy must take into account not only crucial elements within your own walls, but also elements in the external environment that affect your ability to function.

Internally, these include such elements as your organization's mission, vision and values, goals and objectives; your internal stakeholders and their requirements; and the internal composition of your organization—your processes, policies and structures, your intellectual, technical and physical resources, and the capabilities, attitudes and behaviors of your people. It also includes an intangible but vital resource called business capital, which is the value derived from multiple sources and which forms an integral part of your value-driven strategy.

Externally, key elements include various stakeholders—your organization's supply chain and distribution channels, the competitive landscape, the end-user marketplace and other external stakeholders—plus external factors, such as the social, economic and political environment, that affect your business as well as others.

The following briefly describes the key elements, which will be discussed in greater detail in the subsequent chapters.

Stakeholder
A stakeholder is anyone or anything that can influence or be affected by the affairs of your organization. Stakeholders are the primary focus of a value-driven strategy. We discuss stakeholders in depth in Exercise 1: Stakeholder Analysis, then look at their interrelationships in Exercise 2: Stakeholder Network/Community.

Business capital
Business capital is the reservoir of resources and capabilities at your disposal to carry out your value-driven strategy. Business capital must be continuously generated and replenished to ensure a sustainable future. We discuss business capital in depth in Exercise 3: Business Capital Inventory, then look at present and future sources in Exercise 4: Expanded SWOT Analysis.

External factor
An external factor is any aspect of the business environment that can affect your business or that of your stakeholders. External factors are beyond your control; however, to be sustainable, you must anticipate and prepare for their potential impact. We discuss external factors in more detail in Exercise 4: Expanded SWOT Analysis.

Strategic drivers
Strategic drivers are the organizational choices—mission, values, vision, goals and objectives—that define your strategic direction and the path you will follow. We discuss strategic drivers in depth in Exercise 5: Mission, Values and Rules of Engagement, Exercise 6: Envisioning the Future, Exercise 7: Strategy Mapping (objectives), and Exercise 8: Strategic Scorecard (goals).

Internal composition
The internal composition of your organization comprises all of the formal and informal systems, structures, policies, processes, resources and abilities, and the unique way in which they are configured. Your internal composition determines how successful you will be in executing your strategy. We discuss internal composition in detail in Exercise 10: Internal Alignment.

Each of these elements must be considered in turn as you work through the planning steps.

Key Strategic Elements

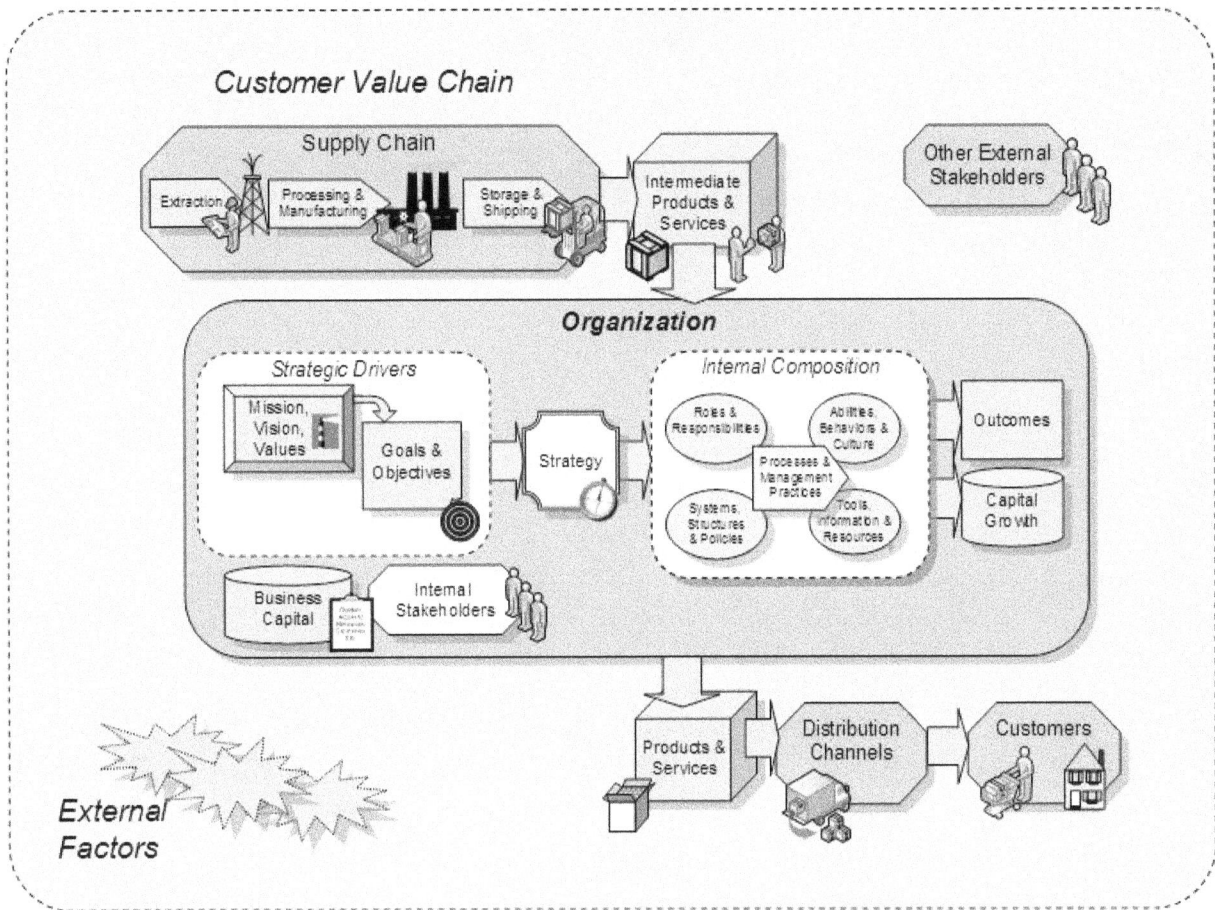

Part I: Strategic Assessment

The first step in planning is to assess where you are now, what challenges you face and what possibilities exist to create a more sustainable future. Who are your stakeholders and what do they need or expect from you? Who is your competition, and how do you stack up against them? What changes are in the wind, and how prepared are you to meet them?

In this section we introduce four analytical exercises that can help your organization address these questions:

- **Exercise 1: Stakeholder Analysis**
  An in depth analysis of your stakeholders—who they are, what they want from you, how they perceive you, how they impact you, and what possibilities may exist for enhancing your relationships

- **Exercise 2: Stakeholder Network/Community**
  An analysis of the interrelationships among your stakeholders and the possibilities for strengthening their ties to your organization

- **Exercise 3: Business Capital Inventory**
  A detailed analysis of the types and sources of business capital and the possibilities for enhancing your capital

- **Exercise 4: Expanded SWOT Analysis**
  A brainstorming exercise that looks ahead into the future to identify possible situations that may arise and to assess their potential impact on your organization

Exercise 1: Stakeholder Analysis

A stakeholder, you'll recall, is anyone or anything that can influence or be affected by the affairs of your organization. Every organization has various constituencies that warrant its attention: owners, investors, customers, employees, creditors, regulators, suppliers, distributors, business partners, competitors, communities, the environment, special interest groups, industry associations, labor unions, and many others.

Each of these constituencies in turn may hold a diverse set of viewpoints among its members, so that it is seldom sufficient to treat them as a single, cohesive unit with identical wants, needs and expectations. Customers, for instance, have a range of needs, based on their individual circumstances and preferences; for instance, some may emphasize convenience and affordability, while others require a customized solution. Likewise, employees expect different things from their employer, based on their lifestyles and circumstances; some may be seeking an opportunity to learn and advance their careers, while others may care most about a steady paycheck and flexible work schedule. Understanding and accommodating these individual differences can enhance the value your organization provides to your stakeholders.

Operational and Other Stakeholders

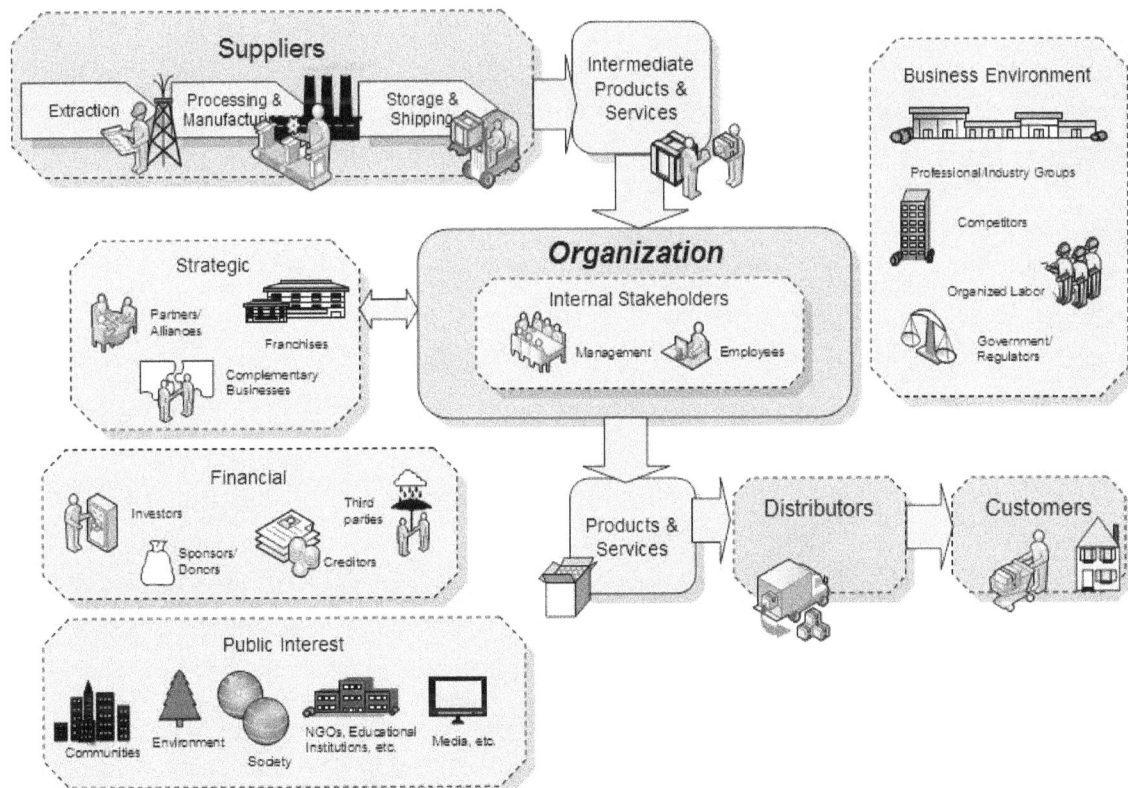

In addition to understanding what your stakeholders want and expect from your organization, you must also understand how they impact your business and what they have to offer in exchange. Perhaps they can refer business to you, share vital information, or provide the necessary licenses, permits and resources to set up shop.

Furthermore, the exchange of value is not solely on a transactional basis; in most cases there is a temporal quality to the exchange that endures over time and forms the basis of a relationship. For example, a grocery store's customers may be willing to pay a higher price on certain items in their shopping basket on any given day because they believe that overall they receive good value for their money—better quality, perhaps, or lower prices on other items—or because they want to ensure that the store remains in business in their neighborhood. A town may grant permission to build a new manufacturing plant in their community in anticipation of new jobs and more business for local suppliers, restaurants and other services.

Exhibit 1 outlines many of the stakeholders of an organization, what they typically value and their potential importance as a source of value to the organization. For discussion purposes they have been grouped into several broad categories: operational, strategic, financial, business environment and public interest. In reality there may be considerable overlap among the groupings; e.g., government regulators represent the public interest as well as helping shape the business environment, while employees may also be customers, shareholders or both.

Exhibit 1: Examples of Stakeholder Value

	Stakeholders	What They May Want	What They Can Provide
I. Operational	A. Clients, customers and prospects	Quality products and services, reliability, convenience, responsiveness	Prompt payment, repeat purchases, referrals, product ideas
	B. Employees and management	Satisfying work, fair wages, good working conditions; recognition, opportunities to advance; power and prestige	Performance of duties, productivity, dependability, honesty, loyalty, flexibility, leadership, innovation
	C. Suppliers	Prompt payment, consistent purchases, fair negotiations	Availability, good terms, responsiveness
	D. Distributors, agents and ancillary services	Reliability, inventory management, priority or exclusivity	Loyalty, promotion assistance
II. Strategic	A. Business partners, alliances	Accountability, transparency, equitable treatment, mutual respect and support, fulfillment of obligations, referrals	Accountability, transparency, equitable treatment, mutual respect and support, fulfillment of obligations, referrals
	B. Franchisors/franchisees	Conformance with standards; guidance, influence, flexibility	Guidance, influence, flexibility; conformance with standards
	C. Complementary enterprises	Coordination of standards, referrals	Coordination of standards, referrals
III. Financial	A. Shareholders, owners and investors	Capital growth, income, degree of influence/control	Source of capital investment, management support
	B. Trustees, sponsors, donors and contributors (to non-profits)	Fulfillment of mission, prudent use of funding, accountability	Financial and/or operational support, reliability, flexibility
	C. Creditors	Timely payment, adherence to terms	Financial support, reasonable terms, flexibility, dependability during hard times
	D. Financial guarantors and third parties	Transparency, risk-adjusted returns	Access to broader markets, risk mitigation
IV. Business environment	A. Government and regulators	Adherence to laws, compliance with regulations, corporate citizenship	Non-interference, supportive programs, protection from unfair competition
	B. Professional, trade and industry associations	Innovation, public image	Knowledge transfer, image
	C. Labor unions	Fair wages, good working conditions, consistency	Fairness, reasonable demands, flexibility
	D. Competitors	Fair business practices, consistency, transparency	Fair business practices, consistency, transparency
V. Public interest	A. Communities	Local jobs, tax revenues, community involvement, protection from harm	Public services, well-trained work force, access to resources, prompt decision-making
	B. Environment	Protection from harm, fair compensation for resource utilization	Access to resources, hospitable conditions
	C. Society	Adherence to cultural norms, accountability, appropriate compensation for resources and infrastructure utilization	Positive recognition
	D. Special interest groups, non-profits, NGOs, educational institutions	Support for core issues, political and financial support,	Mutual support or non-interference
	E. Media, general public, bloggers	Transparency, accountability,, influence	Fairness, respect for privacy

The stakeholder analysis considers the current status of the relationships with your stakeholders and possibilities for enhancing those relationships. As you consider such possibilities, withhold judgment for now to avoid ruling out ideas prematurely. You will have an opportunity to evaluate the ideas during the strategy formulation phase.

As you analyze your stakeholders, you will need to consider the following:

- Who they are
- What they need, want and expect/what matters to them and what drives their behavior
- How they perceive you—your organization, your products and services, and the ways in which you interact with them
- What they can provide/how they impact your business
- Possibilities for enhancing your relationship with them

Realistically, because you don't have unlimited time or resources, you may not be able to conduct an in-depth assessment of every constituent, nor is it necessary. Use your judgment to establish priorities, spending your time and effort accordingly on your most crucial stakeholders. Only you can judge what is appropriate for your organization and how far you need to take the analysis. Nonetheless, at a minimum, try to identify as many distinct stakeholder groups as possible and assess their relative importance to your business over time. In particular, be sure to flag those who may have any negative perceptions of your organization, as these can have a disproportionate and detrimental impact on your business.

To begin the assessment, gather and review everything people within your organization may already know about your stakeholders. Look at customer feedback, employee exit interviews, on-line blogs, sales reports—anything that offers an insight into the concerns and perceptions of your stakeholders. Conduct group interviews of internal staff: purchasers, salespeople, investor relations, compliance officers—anyone who has regular interactions with stakeholders. Then validate your findings and fill in the crucial knowledge gaps through external research, using the best methodologies available within your budget and time constraints. These may include direct observation, focus groups, interviews, surveys, charrettes, advisory panels and so forth.

In the remainder of this chapter, we discuss two operational stakeholder groups—customers and employees—in depth, to illustrate the dimensions and level of detail that you might consider. Due to space limitations, we provide a brief overview of the remaining key groups, which you are encouraged to expand upon with similar levels of detail.

I. Operational Stakeholders

The first group of stakeholders comprises those that are closest to your business and without whom your business would not exist. They include customers, employees, suppliers and distributors—the vital links in your value chain. They are the ones you probably know the most about, although it is always a good idea to test what you think you know and confirm assumptions before making important decisions.

I-A: Clients, customers and prospects

The discussion which follows looks at customers from many different perspectives. Some of these perspectives will be relevant to your organization, others may not. If your organization's customer base is small enough with a diverse set of needs, you may want to conduct the analysis for every single customer. On the other hand, if your customer base is much larger, you will mostly likely need to keep the analysis at a higher level, grouping customers that are similar to each other in terms of their needs and leaving the in-depth analysis, if any, for your sales team. Again, it is up to you to decide what level of analysis is relevant and useful to your organization.

1) Who they are

Most likely, your organization already has some way of segmenting customers, based on certain inherent characteristics. Traditional consumer segments may be based on demographics—household size, age, income, and so forth—and on psychographics—attitudes, cultural affiliations and distinct patterns of behavior. Institutional customers may be segmented along industry lines, sales revenue, geography, and so forth. To the extent possible, each of these segments should be considered separately, as their needs and buying habits may differ in important ways.

For instance, individual investors in the stock market might be classified as either active traders or long term investors. Long-term investors might then be further segmented based on their investable assets, their personal risk profiles and the level of guidance they desire. Some will want an expert to manage their assets for them, while others may want to make their own decisions with or without the help of a financial advisor.

VIPs versus core; customers versus prospects

Customers may be further classified by the nature of their relationship with your organization—VIPs/key accounts, core customers, and prospects—and the number and type of products and services they receive from you.

A common way of ranking customers is by estimating their lifetime economic value to the business, including both accumulated and projected revenues and referral business, less the associated costs, for each customer. While this can be a useful guide, it can also be misleading, and should be used with caution.

- On the plus side, the analysis may reveal that too much or too little time is being spent with specific customers, or that certain relationships are consuming a disproportionate amount of your organization's resources. By adjusting the allocation of resources and finding ways to redress any imbalances, the organization is able to transform high-maintenance, low-margin relationships and to retain and grow healthy ones.

- On the minus side, future revenues might be over- or under-estimated, causing a misallocation of resources. Many salespeople are inherently optimistic about how much business they can generate, while others tend to be more conservative when setting expectations. Sales managers often set overly aggressive targets based on desired levels of growth. These biases may be reflected in the revenue projections used to determine their customers' lifetime value.

- Another potential downside is that future revenues may become the sole driver of relationship activity. As a result, insufficient attention may be given to loyal customers with a strong buying history but low projected revenues going forward. This situation arises whenever a customer has reached product saturation, i.e., they've bought everything you have to offer throughout their organization, or perhaps they have paid a significant lump-sum amount to acquire lifetime rights to your products and services. Because there is little more to be gained in the future from these customers in terms of direct revenue (in the absence of new products), they fall off the radar, despite having been one of your best customers. Lack of attention to these customers can create tremendous backlash, resulting in negative word-of-mouth and a poor public image among other customers and prospects (thereby undermining your business capital – see Exercise 3).

- Lastly and most important, economic lifetime value often overlooks the current and potential non-quantifiable value given to and received from customers, such as testimonials and new product ideas. By contrast, the essence of a value-driven strategy is to include all sources of value, qualitative as well as quantitative, in assessing the lifetime value of the relationship.

What about prospects? Conventional wisdom recognizes that it is more cost-effective to focus on retaining and growing existing customers rather than on acquiring new ones. While that is so, every business faces some level of attrition over time, making it necessary to prospect for new customers. Some businesses, by their very nature, have high customer turnover—wedding planners and universities, for example--and must concentrate on acquiring new customers to replace the old.

The best prospects are typically those who most closely resemble your existing customers. If you have saturated those segments and need to expand into new market segments, you will need to develop a deeper understanding of those new segments, and how they differ from your existing customer base. In either case, a good rule to follow is to treat your best customers like prospects (i.e., don't take them for granted, lest they leave you), and treat your best prospects like customers (i.e., treat them like insiders, so they become one).

One customer, multiple perspectives

Customers may be defined as individual persons or buying centers, or they may be grouped into larger units, such as households or corporate accounts, with multiple potential buyers of your products and services. Whether your customers are retail consumers or institutional buying centers, each purchase decision involves multiple roles played by one or more persons, each with a unique perspective that you must consider during your stakeholder analysis. Typical roles include the following:

- Decision-maker

- Influencer (often someone with technical expertise, though not always)

- User or beneficiary

- Payer

- Support provider (handles care, maintenance and disposal)

Within the retail arena, the possibilities range from the simplest case, involving a single individual playing all relevant roles for a routine purchase, to more complex situations involving several persons, each playing one or more roles. For example:

- An adult routinely getting a haircut, ordering lunch or buying a magazine may be influenced by a spouse's or friend's opinion, but otherwise handles everything—chooses, pays and enjoys the purchase—on his or her own.

- A couple buying a home consider the practical needs of other family members, such as children, pets and elderly parents, and are likely to be influenced by the advice of their realtor, lawyer, home inspector or other professional, as well as by friends, neighbors, colleagues and employers. In addition, the homebuyers may take into account the future resale value of their home, as well as the upkeep of the property. The mortgage lender must approve the purchase, with input from the appraiser, before providing funding.

- A parent whose child requires medical treatment acts on the advice from the child's doctors and other healthcare providers, while the family's health insurance company typically pays for a substantial portion of the care.

In the business-to-business world, other than sole proprietorships, even the simplest purchase typically involves multiple people across several roles. At a minimum, there is usually a purchasing agent and an end user. There may be multiple users, as well as technical advisors, who must agree, and financial gatekeepers who can overrule the decision. In some cases the decision-maker is an active participant throughout the evaluation process; in others, the decision-maker merely ratifies or vetoes the recommendations put forth by others. For example:

- Based on input from staff trainers and a panel of employees representing various subgroups, the VP of Human Resources selects a diversity training program that will be used by various department managers to educate their employees.

- A hospital selects the pharmaceutical products for its formulary; each doctor then chooses the appropriate drug to prescribe for her patient. The patient or his insurance company pays for the drug along with the rest of the in-hospital care.

- A cross-functional task force, including representatives from marketing, sales, IT and Finance, recommends a CRM system for use across the company's lines of business. The Executive Committee makes the final decision. IT handles the installation and system maintenance, while marketing provides customer profiles and campaign data and the sales teams use and update the activity data.

You may wonder why you should worry about these other roles. After all, isn't the decision-maker the one that really matters? The simple answer is no. While the decision-maker is vitally important, her decision may be influenced by others. You increase the odds of a good outcome when you understand the entire decision-making process and can address the concerns each person brings to the table. Even when the decision-maker herself has overlooked one or more perspectives, such as how easy the product will be to use and maintain, you add value by anticipating those perspectives for her and ensuring a more satisfying experience for all customer stakeholders over the useful life of the product.

Your customers' stakeholders

To complete the picture, for those of you whose customers are also businesses in their own right, it behooves you to look through to their ultimate customer, as well as to their other key stakeholders. Are your customers highly dependent on certain suppliers or distribution channels? Are they constrained by obligations to their financial backers or by government regulations? When your organization has a solid understanding of your customers' key stakeholders, you are in the best position to provide additional value to both.

For example, a firm that provides sales training to banks needs to understand what type of customers the bank serves. In addition to serving the typical individual accountholder and borrower, they may offer private banking to high net worth clients and commercial services to local businesses. Money center banks may also have very large corporate clients with specialized needs, such as project financing and investment banking. The selling practices and availability for training will be vastly different for a teller from those of an investment banker, and the content and format of the training will need to address those differences accordingly.

2) What they want, need and expect

In identifying what customers want, need and expect, there are several points to keep in mind:

- What they want, need and expect is complex and varies by person, role and circumstance.

- Products and services are part of a continuum, with considerable overlap.

- Needs are not limited to the product or service itself, but include the entire process surrounding the purchase.

- Needs may be both rational and emotional, and not all are consciously recognized or acknowledged.

- Sometimes wants and needs are defined in the negative, i.e., what they don't want.

- Customers don't always know what they need.

- Not all wants and needs have the same importance.

As you consider these points, identify any gaps that may exist in your products and services and give some thought to the broader range of customers' needs beyond those addressed by your current offerings. Some of your best opportunities may come from addressing their other concerns.

Complexity of needs

It goes without saying that each customer's needs and priorities are uniquely his own, with a unique combination of must-haves and nice-to-haves. What's more, needs and preferences are likely to change as circumstances and perspectives change. For instance, an amateur or novice user wants something that is simple and easy to use, while a professional or expert user typically prefers a sophisticated product with lots of bells and whistles. The user of a product is focused on the functions it is required to perform, while the person holding the purse strings focuses on keeping the cost within budget. While it is impractical to try to anticipate every possible combination of needs and desires for every customer and perspective, it is prudent to consider the range of needs you are likely to encounter across your customer base.

Product-service continuum

The distinction between products and services is somewhat blurred; each contains aspects of the other. What we traditionally think of as a product is in reality a customer-owned means for obtaining one or more services. A service, on the other hand, may involve the same or similar goods as a means of providing the service.

- A vehicle, for example, is a means of transportation. A car might be owned outright (product), rented (service), or leased (also a service, although the customer may feel as if she owns the car, so it feels like a product). If the customer prefers not to drive, she may hire a taxi or limo (services), she may hire a chauffeur (service) to drive her own vehicle (product), or she may choose to use public transit (service).

- A single product may provide multiple services. Phones used to be solely a means of voice communication; today they provide text and visual communication as well, record pictures and video, download music, provide global positioning data, replace airline boarding passes and event tickets, provide instant price and product availability information for shoppers, and offer scores of entertainment options.

As you think about your customers' needs, consider the various choices they have to satisfy those needs and how your current offerings compare. The better you understand the full range of options for satisfying customer needs, the more likely that you will discover new ways to add value.

Beyond the product

Customer needs and preferences are not limited to those pertaining to a product or service itself, but include the entire process surrounding the purchase.

- Prior to making a purchase, the customer may need information or advice, including the opportunity to envision or experience the product or service firsthand, to help guide the selection process.

- During the purchase transaction itself, the customer wants such features as convenient and secure payment and delivery options, information on guarantees and return policies, and a documented record of the transaction.

- Following the purchase, the customer expects timely receipt, easy setup or installation, responsive technical support and complaint resolution, and convenient cancellation, return or exchange options.

At a minimum, customers want the entire process to be as easy and convenient as possible. When the customer is also entertained or educated along the way or given personalized attention, the entire experience can provide added value and satisfy a broader set of needs.

Many companies think about the sales process from their own perspective. Indeed, there is an entire industry focused on teaching salespeople how to plan, prospect and close the sale. The best companies turn the process on its head; instead of focusing on the sales process, they focus on the customer's buying process. When Amazon wanted to compete with bookstores by selling books online, it quickly learned to mimic the in-store experience by enabling customers to digitally thumb through the book, scanning the book jacket and table of contents and reading several pages to get a feel for the author's writing style. Take a closer look at your own customers' buying processes and consider ways in which you could make it easier to do business with you.

Overt and hidden needs

The needs that customers express, called the presenting needs, are often only the tip of the iceberg, so to speak. Presenting needs typically relate to the specific functionality or performance standards that the customer desires, along with aesthetic and cost considerations. Typical presenting needs may include such concerns as the following:

- Suitability for a given purpose
- Conformance with specific technical requirements
- Reliability
- Ease of use and maintenance
- Convenience/speed
- Cost-effectiveness
- Durability
- Technological leadership
- Style
- Safety

Much has been written about hidden needs and subconscious motivations which drive customer buying behaviors. While customers are typically able to articulate practical needs relating to performance and cost, they are less comfortable expressing their psychological needs, such as the need for power, status, affiliation and risk avoidance. This is especially true for institutional clients, where the organizational needs are readily articulated while their own personal needs for status or security may remain unspoken. These hidden motivators can have a significant impact on the buying decision, without ever being acknowledged. Although the customer is unaware of or unable to acknowledge these needs and motivations, it behooves you to recognize them and address them in your strategy, while allowing them to remain unspoken.

Negative needs

Sometimes wants and needs are defined in the negative, i.e., what customers don't want. Factors contributing to customer dissatisfaction are often the little (or big) annoyances that are only noticed when they occur, such as packaging that is difficult to open or automated phone menus that never allow the customer to reach a live person who is both knowledgeable and articulate. Often these dissatisfiers remain unspoken, while they continually erode customer satisfaction and goodwill toward the product or service and its provider. One of the best ways to uncover these negative factors is through observation, either by playing the role of a customer, e.g., mystery shopper, or by direct observation of the product or service during use, e.g., videotaping customers waiting in a queue or assembling and using a product.

Mistaken needs

Another reason to gather insights through direct observation is that people are sometimes mistaken about how they actually do something or what the underlying problem may be. This fact about human behavior became evident during the quality movement, when process consultants discovered that people described their processes one way, but actually performed them another way, often unconscious of the adaptations that had gradually crept into the process. It became an essential precept of the quality movement to observe the work as it was being performed, rather than rely on self-reporting.

Similarly, customers sometimes misdiagnose a problem or assume that they need a particular solution, and only through investigation does the real need become apparent. For example, when sales volume drops despite high levels of inquiry from prospects, the sales manager may assume his salespeople need training in how to close sales, when in fact it is the long wait times due to a supplier bottleneck that is making customers walk away. If you accept the manager's diagnosis and provide the sales training, the real problem won't be solved and he'll assume that the fault lies with your training, not his misdiagnosis. As with hidden needs, it is important to recognize when customers may be mistaken and to find ways to ascertain their real needs while remaining respectful of their views.

Relative importance of wants and needs

Not all customer needs have equal weight; some are must-haves, some are nice-to-haves. It is important to understand the sometimes complex interrelationships that exist among the customer's requirements, with specific thresholds that must be met before other criteria take over. Overly simplistic surveys often ask customers to rank their needs along certain dimensions, e.g., quality, cost, convenience, and so forth; however, this often masks the real priorities among the customers' wants and needs.

For instance, a car buyer may want an affordable vehicle with good mileage, adequate space, and easy handling. If forced to rank these four qualities, he may say price, size, fuel efficiency and handling. In reality, once the price is below a certain budgetary limit, say $30,000, he may choose the more expensive car with greater cargo space, better gas mileage, or four-wheel drive; price is no longer the primary driver. Only after he has satisfied each of his space, efficiency and handling requirements may price come back into play. Failure to recognize these layers of customer priorities can cause the organization to design a product—in this case, a car—that overemphasizes certain needs, such as price, while underemphasizing others, such as space or handling. If the car is cheaply made, too small or rough-handling, it will not even make the list for the buyer's consideration, despite its low sticker price.

3) How they perceive you

As you take stock of your customer relationships, it is important to understand how they perceive you—your organization, your products and services, and the ways in which you interact with them. Your customers' perceptions represent the sum total of their past experiences as well as your reputation among other stakeholders. Like trust, positive perceptions can be lost in an instant, while negative perceptions tend to last a long time. An anecdote from the author's own personal experience provides an example (see first sidebar story on page 23).

But this doesn't mean that there are no second chances. Experience has shown that if an organization does a good job of resolving problems when they arise, as they inevitably will, the experience can leave the customer feeling even more positive than before the problem occurred. (See second sidebar story on page 23.)

Studies of how our memories work suggest that people tend to remember three types of experiences—first impressions, recent events, and those moments associated with a strong emotional response. That is why how you handle problems has such a great impact on the way customers perceive you. Their heightened emotional state when a problem occurs---anger, frustration, anxiety—can leave a lasting negative impression unless the resolution is prompt and fully satisfactory, replacing the negative emotions with a sense of relief, as in the second example.

Customer perceptions of you occur on three levels;

- The organization as a whole
- Your products and services
- The ways in which you interact with them

The organization

The customer's first impression of the organization itself often comes from public sources—the media, your website and advertisements, government agency reviews and so forth. If your organization is known to be a good place to work, is recognized for its ethical behavior in the face of adversity, and plays an active role in the community, the perception will be positive. If, on the other hand, your organization has a reputation for cutting corners, using abusive labor practices, or giving lip service to environmental issues while continuing to pollute, the image will be negative. In particular, if there is any discernable gap between what you say and what you do, you may be seen as untrustworthy, so that even the good things that you do will be discounted or seen as mere whitewashing.

In 1982 Johnson & Johnson received extremely positive media coverage for its prompt and conscientious handling of a crisis involving criminal poisoning of eight bottles of Tylenol, one of its major products. In an extraordinary display of caution on behalf of public safety, the company issued a massive recall of the product, warned hospitals and consumers not to use the product, and offered to exchange tamper-proof tablets for any previously purchased Tylenol capsules. Even though the company bore no responsibility for the product tampering, they provided counseling and financial assistance to the families of the victims who were poisoned. Tylenol suffered a brief but deep slump in demand, only to rebound to become the leading over-the-counter analgesic product several years later. Meanwhile Johnson & Johnson enjoyed a sterling reputation for their handling of the crisis.[2]

Fast forward to 2010 and the story changes. Due to manufacturing deficiencies that resulted in potential contamination, Johnson & Johnson was compelled to recall over forty over-the-counter products, including several products for infants and children. Because these recalls, although voluntary, occurred only gradually and because the company was reported as having initially removed the products from shelves surreptitiously without informing the public, there was considerable criticism levied against the company. Furthermore, because the products potentially affected children, the public response was all the more emotionally charged. Ultimately, the company was brought under investigation by both Congress and the FDA, leaving its formerly pristine reputation significantly tarnished.[3]

Until the earlier crisis occurred, Johnson & Johnson did not have a strong public relations program; their relationship with the media and their public image were based largely on product marketing and advertising. The media coverage that followed provided a window into the company's core values, something that could not be discerned from their product marketing alone. Even in today's world of instantaneous news and internet blogs, how your customers perceive you may be similarly constrained by the information that is publicly available. As you think about your customers, ask yourself how well they know your organization and what perceptions they might have that are inaccurate and potentially harmful. Then think about what you can do to change those perceptions.

---

[2] Source: www.ou.edu/deptcomm/dodjcc/groups/02C2/Johnson%20&%20Johnson.htm
3 Sourceswww.npr.org/blogs/health/2010/05/27/127209969/johnson-johnson;
www.fda.gov/NewsEvents/Testimony/ucm213640.htm

Paradise Lost

My Dell laptop had been a faithful companion for several years, but was becoming obsolete as newer versions of essential software required increasing amounts of memory. This was especially limiting my ability to work online. Although I loved the laptop, I finally gave in to the need to replace it. Happy with Dell, this time I vowed to buy their most powerful computer available, with all the bells and whistles, opting for a desktop rather than laptop so its memory could be more easily upgraded. It was expensive, but I was convinced it was a worthwhile investment.

The problems began right away. Although I had paid Dell to have my data files transferred from the laptop to the new desktop, the technician informed me that, due to different ports and media readers, the two computers could not communicate with one another, despite both being Dell computers. He stated that there were no cables or media that would enable him to download the files from the laptop and upload them to the desktop.

Seriously distressed by the news, I called Dell customer service with the intention of returning the desktop. However, the customer service representative, who spoke limited English, insisted that this was not a customer service issue and that I must speak with technical support. Exasperated after several attempts to seek resolution, I gave up on returning the computer or getting a refund for the non-provided data transfer service. But my troubles had only just begun.

I spent the first week laboriously recreating the essential files that I needed from the laptop. The desktop was noticeably faster, especially when online, and I was able to use a broader range of features. Just as I was getting comfortable that I had what I needed, the hard drive crashed. Nothing I did seemed to help, so I called Dell technical support. Over the next few weeks I spent over thirty hours on the phone speaking with tech support in Mumbai, trying to diagnose and resolve the problem. Although I was assigned a technician to work with, twice during the ordeal they were reassigned and I had to start over with a different technician. Although more conversant than the customer service folks had been, none of the technicians was native English-speaking, so we had to work through some communication issues each time.

Adopting a trial-and-error approach, they sent several replacement parts, each of which came with an invoice, in accordance with a Dell policy that only when they had received the original defective part would I receive credit against the invoice. However, the replacement parts made no difference. Exhausted after thirty hours and three different technicians over several weeks, I gave up. My $6,000 investment had lasted all of seven days.

To say that I felt a great degree of frustration and anger toward Dell would be an understatement. Even now, years later, as I relive the memory of that experience, I can feel the emotions rising to the surface. For a long time I wanted nothing more than to smash the computer to bits and send the pieces cash-on-delivery to Dell's founder and president. I had met Michael Dell at a Planning Forum meeting years before, when his new company was being touted as the business model of the future. Not for this former customer. Barring some miraculous turn of events, I will never buy a Dell product again. Not ever.

Paradise Found

In a far less dramatic example than the Dell story, last year I purchased a number of Christmas gifts from amazon.com and had them sent to my family's house in another state, where I would be spending the holidays. In the same order, I also bought some drapes for myself from one of their vendors, Springfield Bedding, but forgot to specify a different shipping address. Realizing my mistake a few hours later, I immediately logged back on to amazon and requested the change in shipping address. I received confirmation from both the vendor and amazon that the correction had been made. Relieved that I would not have to pay to re-ship the drapes from my family's house, I thought no more about it.

Despite the confirmation, however, the drapes were nonetheless sent to the wrong place. When I reported this back to amazon and the vendor, the vendor apologized and offered to either send a second set or pay for the additional shipping cost to re-ship the original package. Since the drapes cost $40 and the shipping had cost only $10, I said that the $10 shipping cost would be fine. The vendor voluntarily decided to issue a credit of $20 instead, to compensate for the delay as well as the out-of-pocket expense. Wow! And it had been my oversight in the first place. You can bet that I will buy from Springfield Bedding again whenever the occasion arises, and encourage others to do so as well.

The products and services

In the absence of evidence to the contrary, customers' impression of your organization will carry over to your products and services—what's commonly known as the "halo effect." So if you are seen as a reputable company, they will assume that your products and services are reliable and effective. On the contrary, if you are seen in a negative light, your products and services will be considered suspect.

Direct experience may tell a different story, however, and the perceptions customers have of your products and services may be different from that of your organization as a whole. You may have a sterling reputation as an organization, but your products must still stand on their own. Apple Computer is a company typically held in high regard as a technological innovator, yet the iPhone 4 was plagued with reception problems in the early days after its launch in 2010. That same year Toyota, a company widely recognized for its leadership in product quality, was forced to recall thousands of vehicles due to a rash of accidents resulting from sudden acceleration. Subsequent study may have exonerated the electronic control system, but the image of product excellence was noticeably tarnished.

Alternatively, a company with superior products can sometimes get away with a less-than-perfect reputation as an organization. For instance, Nike was reported to engage in unfair labor practices overseas, even while its athletic footwear were in high demand. However, when acceptable alternatives are available, the organization's less-than-stellar reputation becomes a factor and may remain so long after the negative press fades from the news. BP experienced a severe backlash after the 2010 deepwater oil leak in the Gulf, as irate car owners boycotted BP gas stations (even though the stations were not actually owned by BP.)

The interactions

The third level on which customers perceive you is the way in which you interact with them, whether face-to-face or remotely, or both. Every contact, whether initiated by you or by the customer, is an opportunity to either build a bond or destroy one. If the customer initiates the contact, he expects a prompt and courteous response which addresses his question or concern directly. Anything less can leave the customer feeling frustrated and resentful. If your organization initiated the contact, the customer expects it to be relevant and timely; otherwise, it will be seen as intrusive and self-serving.

Whenever business is conducted person-to-person, it is often the personal relationship with the people within your organization that is most important in determining whether the customer does business with you. Indeed, often a client will continue to do business with her stockbroker or insurance agent with whom she is comfortable, even when that agent changes firms. No matter how important the customer may be to your organization, the nature of the relationship is defined through the customer's eyes. Until a personal relationship develops with one or more of your people, she may see you merely as a vendor, regardless of the quality of your products or the reputation of your organization. Only when the relationship has progressed to a point where she regards you as a personal ally and trusted business partner will a bond of loyalty be formed.

When the only contact with the customer is through an automated phone system, mail or electronic means, that personal loyalty does not exist. Instead you must build a bond by ensuring that your products and services are flawless and that every contact adds value to the customer's experience with you. Savvy companies make an effort to find out how customers want to be contacted—how often, through what media, with what type of content—and then ensure that everyone in the organization adheres to those guidelines. Likewise, they ensure that their automated phone system always includes the option to speak with a live representative and, if the projected wait time is unacceptable, allows the customer to request and receive a callback at a specific time. Each of these touch points contributes to the customer's overall perception of you and your business.

The number and type of touch points is an important consideration for customers. Customers often prefer one mode of contact over another, and they usually want to be able to choose the mode of contact at any given moment. Customers with regular contact with your organization are apt to want a single point of contact or an expedited mode of contact, such as a direct phone number to their assigned representative. In particular they want consistency and the assurance that details of their relationship with you are known and understood by everyone with whom they interact. When customers must explain themselves repeatedly or when information they have provided is ignored or lost, they may feel alienated and are unlikely to value their relationship with you.

Think about the people and processes that touch your customers. Who, if anyone, manages the total customer relationship? What avenues exist for customers to provide feedback to decision-makers? How much do senior managers know about the full range of customers and their issues? Make note of any gaps and think about how you could address them.

Why it matters

You may wonder why customers' perceptions are so important. For any but the simplest products and services that can be evaluated directly, customers must rely upon their impressions of you and your competition to decide what products and services to buy. The greater the price tag, the more crucial these impressions are. Services by their very nature are intangible, so the customer has no way to directly assess how well they will perform. Many products as well are difficult to assess directly, despite their tangible nature, even after the fact. For example, a customer may enjoy a meal at a restaurant, but have no idea what the nutritional content is or how clean the kitchen was where it was prepared. Or a computer user may not know for certain whether the firewall on his computer is fully protecting his privacy.

Because of the difficulty in evaluating products and services directly, customers must instead rely upon other sources for assurance—tangible clues, personal experience, referrals from people they trust, and reviews by credible experts.

- *Tangible clues*—the customer relies upon appearances to predict performance, for instance, a place of business, such as a restaurant, retail store or law office, may be judged by the quality of their facilities and the appearance and demeanor of their employees and clientele.

- *Personal experience*—the customer expects performance to be similar to what was experienced previously from this provider, even though the product or circumstances may be different, e.g., the contractor who did a great job installing new kitchen cabinets may be hired to build a backyard deck or remodel the bath.

- *Referrals and testimonials*—the customer relies on word-of-mouth or endorsements by respected sources, e.g., he may ask a coworker or neighbor to recommend a tax accountant or landscape architect, or choose a product endorsed by a trusted spokesperson.

- *Credibility*—the customer relies upon the judgment of others with expertise and knowledge of the specific product or service, e.g., government and industry rating agencies, consumer product reviewers, local inspectors and so forth.

Another reason perceptions are so important is that an unhappy customer is more likely than a satisfied customer to tell others about his experience. Whether he tells the company is less certain. If you are fortunate enough to hear from a dissatisfied customer, you have an opportunity to win that customer's gratitude and respect by addressing his complaint quickly and graciously. The recovery process should not be left to chance; it should be well thought out in advance and ingrained in your customer service practices.

As you think about your customers' perceptions of you, consider whether they are well-founded or based on misleading evidence or faulty assumptions, and what corrective actions you may wish to take. Also, give some thought to whether their perceptions are positive, negative, mixed or unknown, and how strongly they feel about those perceptions. In particular, identify those customers who are either strong advocates or detractors of your organization. You will want to leverage the former and neutralize or convert the latter.

4) What they can provide/how they impact your business

Not surprisingly, customers, for the most part, are good for your business. After all, without customers, you would have no business. That having been said, some customers are better than others when it comes to the long term success of your organization. The best customers are the ones who are strong advocates, returning to do business with you again and again, and encouraging others to do the same. Unless they demand an exorbitant amount of your scarce resources, they are likely to be quite profitable as well as beneficial in other ways. They'll tell you what you're doing right, as well as what you need to improve.

The worst customers, on the other hand, are the ones who are detractors, who demand far more than they are willing to pay for or complain about you to others, but never to you. Customers who fall somewhere in between, even though they may be satisfied with you and your products, are easily lured away by other offers; hence their value to you is apt to be short-lived, limited to the occasional transaction and, at best, a superficial relationship. Customer relationships allowed to languish in this way represent a missed opportunity to create added value, both for them and for your organization.

More revenue, lower cost

What are some of the ways customers can provide more value to your business? The most obvious answer is to do more business with you. Additional business could mean buying more of the same products from you at a time, buying more frequently or for longer periods of time, adding other household members or buying centers, or buying additional products and services from you. The latter is especially desirable, as studies have shown that customers who buy multiple products from you tend to be more loyal.

Another way customers can enhance their value to your business is by consuming fewer of your scarce resources, thereby reducing your costs. Customers who are well-informed and organized, and who are comfortable doing things for themselves—e.g., bag their own groceries, pump their own gas—and using technology—e.g., place orders online, receive electronic statements—make it easy to do business with them. The savings go right to your bottom line.

Referrals, testimonials and endorsements

Customers tend to know others who are similar to them in many ways, making them an excellent source of referrals to like-minded prospects for your business. Sometimes those referrals will come informally, through word-of-mouth. While those are great to have, you may not ever know where they came from, unless the new customer tells you. Even better are the referrals that are made with your knowledge, enabling you to track and acknowledge the value thus generated. Asking for referrals needs to be done with grace and tact, and is best done when the customer has just completed a particularly satisfying transaction with you. Depending on the situation, the customer may prefer to have you contact the referral or to handle it themselves. Anytime you receive a referral from a known source, it is important that you acknowledge and thank the customer, regardless of whether the referral proved fruitful.

Customers who have had a positive experience doing business with you may be willing to issue a testimonial on your behalf. The testimonial should highlight some aspect of the experience to help it come alive for the reader, whether spoken, in print or on your website or blog. Endorsements are similar to testimonials, but usually come from someone with greater recognition among prospective customers and may involve a commitment to participate in actively promoting the product or business.

Feedback and ideas

Customers can provide significant value to your business by offering feedback on existing products and services and sharing ideas for new or enhanced ones. In addition to informal discussions with your customer contact people, they may participate in structured interviews, focus groups or surveys. Knowledgeable customers representing key market segments may be invited to take part in an advisory panel on a rotational basis, reviewing concepts and issues of crucial importance to the business. They may be asked to test out new products prior to their release and provide important insights on usability, clarity of instructions, and potential enhancements. Depending on the circumstances, they may be required to sign confidentiality agreements to do so.

Other

Other ways for customers to provide value include such initiatives as lending their support with local communities, regulators, labor unions and other stakeholders and, for business clients: co-marketing or joint advertising; providing information about their business, including projected purchases, their buying process and logistics; and providing on-site space for your representatives to facilitate ongoing interactions and foster deeper understanding of their business.

5) How you can enhance your relationships

By now you have developed a deeper appreciation for who your customers are and what they want, how they perceive you and how they can affect your business. Along the way you may have had flashes of insight into possibilities for improvement. Now is the time to bring it all together and to consider ways to better serve their needs and strengthen your relationships. At this point there is no need to decide which ideas you will implement; the objective here is simply to identify possibilities for further consideration later.

Understand and acknowledge their perspective

First and foremost, you can demonstrate to customers that you truly understand their needs and concerns and that you take them seriously. It may seem obvious, even trivial, but it's a small thing that can make a big difference. It can be as simple as taking time to listen to a request or complaint and then confirming your understanding before offering a response. Or it can mean preparing marketing materials and instructional guides using their language and avoiding unfamiliar terminology.

Address gaps

Equally obvious is addressing any gaps you have uncovered between your existing products and services and their needs. Think about ways to improve your competitive positioning by optimizing the must-haves, eliminating dissatisfiers and addressing the hidden needs that customers cannot articulate. Similarly, look at ways to improve the interactions with your customers at every stage of the buying process. From pre-sale information-gathering to ordering and payment to post-sale delivery and service, there is a multitude of ways to make it easy to do business with you.

Provide ancillary services

When your products and services are the best they can be, there may be other opportunities to enhance their value by providing ancillary services. For instance, a homeowner's insurance provider might include with the policy an electronic household inventory checklist, a digital camera and/or a receipt scanner to document purchases, a protective pouch for important papers, and an emergency guide for use during and after a natural disaster. A retirement plan sponsor might provide information on places to retire, including weather, cost of living, local taxes, housing options, medical care, maintenance services, and educational, recreational and cultural activities.

Address unfilled needs

As you learned more about your customers, you may have discovered needs that are largely unmet in the marketplace. These needs may be peripherally related to your existing products and services, may reflect untapped markets for existing products and services, or may be wholly new. A shuttle service that serves public transit commuters in a bedroom community may choose to provide concierge services as well, including pickup and delivery of dry cleaning, grocery shopping, flowers and greeting cards, and so forth. A company that provides restaurants with the plastic discs that tell diners when their table is ready may find a new market in the waiting rooms of doctors' offices.

Improve perceptions authentically

Another way you can enhance your relationships with customers is to improve their perceptions of you and your products and services. It means fixing the things that ought to be fixed, such as a poor environmental track record or faulty product. It also means communicating more effectively and honestly about what works well and what does not, and what you are doing about the latter. This does not mean whitewashing by pretending to be something you are not. Because of a tendency among consumers to be suspicious of corporate self-promotion, this must be done with extreme care; you must be willing to be placed under close scrutiny by objective third parties if you want to be taken seriously.

I-B: Employees and management

The relationship between employers and employees continues to evolve, away from the paternalistic organization providing long term job and financial security toward a leaner, more entrepreneurial work environment in which performance and internal connections are key drivers of an employee's perceived value. In addition, other trends continue to influence the world of work:

- The nature of work is transforming from industrial to a service and knowledge economy.

- A middle class is emerging in developing countries, bringing both a more educated workforce and greater consumer demand.

- The younger generation is entering the workforce with different values and expectations than the generations preceding them.

- Accelerating technology advances are changing the ways in which we communicate, learn and collaborate.

All of these forces are reshaping the work environment. Corporate restructurings, downsizing and outsourcing are commonplace; 401(k)s have replaced corporate pensions; variable pay has become a more significant part of compensation. The net effect, for all but the topmost executives, has been to shift a greater share of personal financial risk from the employer to the employee.

1) Who they are

Executives often refer to their employees as the organization's most valuable resources. Despite the apparent contradiction whenever downsizings occur, their pronouncement is truer than many realize. In the knowledge economy, much of an organization's capital is embedded in the skills, knowledge and aptitudes of its people. Theories abound regarding how best to manage an organization's workforce; we will not attempt to address those here. Instead, we suggest only that you consider carefully what skills, knowledge and aptitudes are vital to your organization, and who within the organization possesses those valuable capabilities. Look beyond the functional titles and hierarchical levels; the best talent may lie deep within your organization.

The discussion which follows looks at employees from many different perspectives. Some of these perspectives will be relevant to your organization, others may not. Again, it is up to you to decide what level of analysis is relevant and useful to your organization.

Traditional categories

Your organization may have many levels and specialized functions, or it may be fairly flat with broader, more fluid job assignments. In either case, some of the traditional distinctions may still apply. The most fundamental distinction is between staff employees and management; staff may be further distinguished between exempt and non-exempt, based on their pay structure and scope of decision-making, while management may be further categorized by supervisory, team leadership, middle management, and senior executives. Other distinctions may be based on level of education, professional certification, functional expertise or skill level.

Work arrangements

Traditionally most staff members have been full time, permanent employees. While many still fit the traditional profile, there are many other work arrangements that have become more common today. Some positions may be held by contract workers, others by temporary staff through an outside agency. Some employees may work part time, or participate in a job sharing arrangement. Other members of your workforce may include interns or volunteers.

Employees who work traditional 9 to 5 business hours have different requirements than those on flex-time, while shift workers and those on call outside of normal business hours have their own unique needs. Telecommuters, employees in remote locations and those who travel extensively will have different needs from employees based at company headquarters. Especially important is the distinction between unionized and non-union workers. Each of these subgroups is apt to have different expectations and value to your business.

Diversity

An important source of differentiation among employees in terms of their needs and expectations is demographic—age, gender, sexual orientation, family structure, culture and lifestyle—as well as career stage and length of tenure with your organization. Empty nesters will have very different concerns from those of single parents; millennials will differ from baby boomers, immigrants from native-born, expatriates from foreign nationals, long term employees from recent hires. Employees with temporary or permanent disabilities, or whose family members are disabled, will have special needs and concerns of their own.

Past and future workforce

Although we tend to think of our workforce as those in our current employ, there are other pre-and-post-employment stakeholders that should be considered as well, as their needs and potential impact on our business are different still.

Retirees and other former employees may remain connected to the organization through ongoing benefits, including health insurance and retirement plans. Employees who have been downsized sometimes form their own alumni group for networking and moral support; these groups and individuals may maintain ongoing relationships with their former colleagues who remain in your employ, and their perceptions of your organization and how you have treated them can spread by word-of-mouth and affect your public image.

On the other hand, recruitment candidates, whether recent graduates or experienced professionals at other organizations, begin forming their own perceptions of your organization long before you realize that they are candidates. A welcoming website and a transparent, respectful hiring process can go a long way in creating a favorable impression of your organization as a desirable employer.

Overlapping roles

Workers are not just employees; they and their family members may be stakeholders in other ways as well. Whether through retirement plans, ESOPs or other means, they and their families may be shareholders. If your business is consumer-focused, they may also be customers. They are apt to be voters in the local community and may belong to environmental or other special interest groups. These overlapping relationships may be reinforcing, or they may represent conflicting objectives—going the extra mile for customers versus maintaining work-life balance, doing more with less at work versus driving stock appreciation—that the employee must reconcile.

2) What they need, want and expect

It has been said that people either live to work or work to live. For most people it is some combination of both. To provide for themselves and their loved ones, your employees need to earn a living. In the absence of job security with one employer, they must therefore strive to ensure their own employability throughout their working lives.

Once they have addressed their financial security, most seek to spend their time doing work that they find fulfilling, in a safe, comfortable environment. What that means will be different for each individual, but typically will include many of the elements outlined below.

Financial well-being

First and foremost, active employees (other than volunteers and interns) want a steady paycheck, whether that paycheck is expected to provide a basic living wage or supports a higher standard of living. Predictability is important because it enables your employees to make financial commitments to rent a home, obtain a mortgage, buy a car, pay college tuition, and so forth. As mergers, outsourcing, off-shoring and downsizing become increasingly common, employees cannot help but worry about the possibility of job loss. You can help alleviate those concerns by clarifying your policies regarding these practices and demonstrating a commitment to seek less drastic alternatives—furloughs, temporary reductions in wages or benefits, voluntary layoffs or retirement, job-sharing, shorter hours or work weeks—during times of economic turmoil.

While gainfully employed, workers expect their base compensation to cover their day-to-day living expenses, with enough left over to provide for discretionary purchases as well as savings and investments. They also expect their income to keep pace with inflation and, preferably, to grow faster so that they can enjoy an ever-increasing standard of living. Those who are permanently or temporarily out of work—retirees, laid-off workers, injured or sick workers—want continued income protection as well, through retirement plans, severance packages, unemployment benefits, workers' compensation and disability benefits.

Beyond a steady paycheck, many workers appreciate the opportunity to earn additional income, through overtime, commissions, bonuses and other forms of variable compensation. Whether it comes through individual or team-based performance bonuses, pay-for-knowledge, gain-sharing or profit-sharing, they expect the payout to reflect their own individual contributions and abilities. Experienced workers may seek additional forms of financial compensation as well, such as signing bonuses and stock options.

For many workers, a close second to compensation is affordable health insurance. As healthcare costs continue to escalate, more and more families are confronted with the possibility of financial ruin should they experience serious health issues. Workers often choose a job, or remain in a job, solely to obtain the necessary health insurance for themselves and their loved ones. Depending on their circumstances, they may also desire coverage for domestic partners, adult children or siblings, other family members, and persons with pre-existing conditions or mental health issues. Families with chronic conditions may also need coverage for their prescription drugs. The broader your insurance plan, the greater your ability to attract and retain workers with these special needs.

Beyond the availability of health insurance, flexibility in choosing the right coverage is paramount. Some employees prefer a lower premium with a higher deductible, while others prefer the reverse. All other things being equal, most people prefer to keep their existing healthcare providers; however, given that their providers may fall outside their health plan's approved network, they want the flexibility to choose a less expensive alternative. Once they have selected a plan and chosen their healthcare providers, they want to maintain those relationships to ensure continuity of care. Because any time you change the available insurance options, you risk disrupting those relationships, you would do well to make those changes only when necessary.

Less immediate but an equally important concern for most employees is some form of retirement plan to complement or replace the ever-more-tenuous federal Social Security program. Traditional pensions, while most desirable from employees' point of view, are few and far between. Defined benefit plans have largely been replaced by defined contribution plans, shifting both the primary funding and the investment risk onto employees. With that as a given, your employees want you to provide matching funds, access to objective financial guidance, a consistent and balanced range of investment options, and convenient access to their account information. They also want to be able to access their funds whenever necessary (through loans or early withdrawal) and, contrary to most retirement plans, to control when and how their investment options change. As with health insurance, that means you should try to maintain the same plan provider whenever possible and provide portability, so they may remain in the plan after they leave your employ. Those close to or at retirement are most concerned with their ability to receive guaranteed income at sufficient levels, without outliving their income; as life expectancy continues to lengthen and entitlement programs risk running out of funds, this becomes an increasing concern for all.

Other benefits

In addition to adequate compensation, health insurance and a retirement plan, workers desire a wide range of other benefits, depending on their particular circumstances and lifestyle. These benefits may include financial saving accounts, other health and wellness programs, paid time off, life insurance, discount stock purchase plans, family care, transportation assistance, and numerous other categories. A sample listing is provided in Exhibit 2 on the following page.

Exhibit 2: Sample Employee Benefits (adapted from humanresources.about.com)

Medical and Health	Paid Time Off	Other Insurance and Retirement
• On-site medical clinic • Medical care programs (HMO, health insurance) • Dental care programs • Vision care programs • Flexible spending accounts for healthcare costs • Employee assistance programs • Wellness programs • On-site fitness facilities • Fitness facility membership • $xx to take annual physical; $xxx reward if vital signs are positive	• Sick leave • Well pay • Mental health days • Holidays • Vacation • Bereavement leave • XX paid hours a month for volunteer work • Extra vacation days in milestone years • Personal or emergency business days or floating holidays • Paid sabbaticals • Professional association participation	• Short-term disability insurance • Long-term disability insurance • Life insurance • Mental health insurance • Travel accident insurance (when traveling on company business) • Defined benefit pension • Defined contribution • Financial planning assistance • 401(k) • Profit sharing • Discount stock purchase plans
Education and Development	**Transit**	**Children and Family**
• Tuition reimbursement or payment for seminars and classes • Educational assistance (interest-free loans for own or children's education) • Career planning and development • Scholarships for children of employees • Professional association meeting, conference or seminar expense	• Van-pool programs • Company car • Free or subsidized mass-transit passes • Free parking (car or bicycle) • Free taxi rides home • First-class travel • Free ride in jump seat of company planes • Free airline passes • Keep frequent flyer miles for personal use	• Free child care • On-site child care • Free elder care • Vouchers to help pay for child care • Information about cost and quality of day care • Discounts on day care • Flexible spending account for child care • Sick child care center • Financial support for infertility treatments and/or adoption aid
Benefits Related to Pets	**Food and Drink**	**Clothing**
• On-site kennel service • Dog and cat grooming • Animal sitting for business travelers • Pet walking services • Bereavement period for the loss of pets • Pet insurance • Bring a pet to work day • Allowed to keep pets at work	• Free soft drinks, coffee, tea, juice • Free or discount meals/snacks • Cafeteria/snack bar on site • Holiday turkeys • Prepared take-home meals • Paid mini-bar snacks while traveling • Paid meals for entire family if working on weekend (to allow family time) • Food and drinks at company events	• Free uniforms or uniform cleaning • Free clothes for personal use (such as shirts, sweaters, jackets, hats) • Shoe repair • Safety shoes • Safety eyeglasses
Concierge Services	**Personal Care**	**Discounts**
• Car wash and oil change • Dry cleaning service • Maid service to clean home • Errands run	• Beautician/barber/shoeshine on site • Discount haircuts • Free on-site massages • Nap time during the workday	• Leased automobiles • Life insurance • Discounts of closing costs in the purchase of a new home • Clothing
Other Types of Benefits	**Recreation and Entertainment**	**Special Benefits**
• Employee referral bonus • Boomerang bonus (rehire bonus) • Award or gift certificates • Birthday card or note from executive • Prepaid legal services • On site banking services • Life Cycle account to help employees cross major thresholds (buying a first house or financing college education)	• Game rooms (pool, foosball, video games, etc.) • Free movies • Company sponsored/subsidized events • Theme days (e.g., costume parties and holiday cookie or gift exchanges) • Condominium, hotel, camping or other recreational area for employee use	• Relocation expenses • Subsidized or free housing • Annual family trips back to the "home country" of H1 B visa employees • Relocation back to the "home country" if the job doesn't work out or in case of "no fault" layoff or termination • Assistance in obtaining a visa to visit the United States

Working conditions

When it comes to working conditions, two primary concerns for active workers are the work schedule—total hours, time of day, number and length of breaks, paid time off—and work location—distance from home; proximity to restaurants, transportation, shopping and other services or activities; telecommuting; travel requirements, and so forth. The greater the degree of flexibility employees have, the greater their ability to balance work and other demands on their time. Likewise for candidates, who may have constraints on their availability, flexibility in scheduling interviews is important and reflects favorably on you as a potential employer.

Equally important is the comfort and safety of the work environment, the surrounding neighborhood and commuting routes. Safety concerns include protection from injury, illness, crime, and natural or man-made disasters, as well as protection of privacy in the workplace. Comfort may be both physical—lighting, temperature, air quality, noise level, cleanliness and ergonomics—and psychological—freedom from harassment and undue stress, pleasant surroundings, a flexible dress code, and the ability to control one's workspace. All of these factors have significant impact on employee satisfaction, wellness and productivity, as does the suitability of the work environment to the nature of the task at hand—individual or teamwork, private or public, structured or unstructured. By providing a clean, safe, comfortable work environment, adaptable to the individual and the work being done, you help foster productivity while reducing absenteeism and employee turnover.

Meaningful work

Although satisfactory conditions and financial wellbeing are necessary, job satisfaction doesn't come merely from a paycheck or comfortable work environment. True job satisfaction comes from doing work that has personal meaning to the individual doing the work and that produces or makes progress toward a desired result. Certain characteristics are typical of work that employees find meaningful and intrinsically motivating:

- The work is framed in such a way as to give it a sense of purpose that aligns with the worker's value system and supports the organization's strategic objectives—for instance, a construction worker is not just laying asphalt, but building a safer highway; a volunteer is not just stuffing envelopes for a fundraising campaign, but helping feed the hungry. The employee feels a part of something bigger than themselves.

- The work is challenging without being daunting—the employee has a clear objective and the necessary skills and resources, and is capable of achieving the objective with a gentle stretch just beyond her comfort zone. The employee derives a sense of mastery by meeting the challenge.

- The employee has a sense of autonomy, with ultimate control over the how the work is done, yet with guidance and support commensurate with her skill level.

- Whether an effort initially succeeds or fails, the employee feels a sense of accomplishment for the learning that occurs and the increased likelihood of future success. Failure is treated as a shared learning opportunity by both the employee and the organization.

Respect and self-esteem

Employees' attitudes and behaviors tend to reflect the way in which they are treated. Your employees want to be able to trust you and want to be treated as trustworthy in return. If you consider them trustworthy, responsible adults, they typically will behave as such, taking initiative and getting things done. However, if you regard them as lazy and untrustworthy, in need of constant monitoring and micro-managing, they are likely to cease taking initiative and to do only the minimal amount required of them. Even the most conscientious employees, while continuing to hold themselves to higher standards, may feel alienated and disinclined to offer their best ideas. Similarly, if employees are given free rein without accountability, they are more likely to take advantage and place their own personal interests ahead of yours.

The best managed organizations go out of their way to demonstrate high ethical standards, foster open communications with employees and hold themselves and employees accountable. They do not punish honest mistakes but treat them as learning opportunities. They balance concerns for security and employee safety with concerns for individual privacy, limiting their intrusion into employee activities. They handle rejection of candidates, employee dismissals and other employee matters with tact and sensitivity, providing honest feedback while protecting employees' dignity and self-esteem.

Employees also want to know that you respect them for who they are, regardless of their race, gender, nationality, sexual orientation, religion, age, marital status, or culture. They want to know that you appreciate diversity and welcome different perspectives, that you do not tolerate discriminatory behavior toward any employee, and that you understand their unique needs and concerns. Unless they see those policies demonstrated in everyday management practices and decisions, they will disregard official policy statements as mere lip service.

Your employees expect to be treated fairly, both in terms of balancing your needs with their own and in terms of equitable treatment with their colleagues. If you place unreasonable demands on them, expect them to work consistently long hours or to take on added uncompensated work due to reductions in staff, or otherwise persist in placing organization needs ahead of theirs, you will quickly erode their trust. While employees understand that there may be times when you must ask more of them than usual, they want to know that you recognize the added burden you are placing on them and that you are willing to actively seek both to mitigate the impact and to compensate them appropriately.

Likewise, they expect to be treated fairly in relation to other employees. Perceptions of fairness are based not only on the outcomes—who got the promotion or plum assignment, how is each person compensated—but also on the way in which the decisions are made. If the decision seems arbitrary or subjective, with little or no opportunity for employee input, those for whom the outcome was unfavorable are bound to be resentful, while the winner may feel guilty and subsequently ostracized by their peers. If the decision was based on clear, objective criteria and employee input was solicited, most employees are apt to accept the outcome with little adverse reaction.

Growth opportunities

No matter what stage of their career they are in, employees need to continue to learn and grow. New hires in general, and interns in particular, are seeking real world work experience to build their skills and knowledge, develop professional contacts, and explore specific fields or work environments to determine the best fit. Experienced workers desire advancement opportunities that will provide them with greater responsibilities and, perhaps, bigger titles as they move up the organizational hierarchy. However, as organizations become flatter and the baby boomer generation reaches the final stage of their careers, the supply of management positions no longer meets the demand. Instead, personal growth must come either by broadening skills through lateral moves or by deepening expertise within one's chosen field.

At the same time, rapid advances in technology require a continuous cycle of learning for everyone, as skills and knowledge are quickly rendered obsolete. Unless your organization recognizes the emerging needs and provides appropriate training and development opportunities on a regular basis, you are likely to face an increasing challenge to maintain a productive workforce. On the other hand, if you consistently provide opportunities to learn and apply leading edge skills, you will be rewarded with lower turnover and more engaged, committed employees.

Employees' desire to learn and grow goes well beyond their current employment. Lacking the job security of the past, employees are increasingly concerned about maintaining their employability. Those with professional licenses want adequate time and resources to maintain their certification through continuing education and payment of licensing fees. Others may want to take outside courses, whether degree-based or continuing education, to broaden or deepen their skills and knowledge. Even when these courses have little or no bearing on their current position, providing the time flexibility and tuition assistance can be a wise investment, as it enhances job satisfaction and goodwill toward the company, stimulates creativity, and contributes toward both increased productivity and improved retention.

Nowhere is the need for assistance with personal development felt more keenly than among the recently dislocated or unemployed. People whose jobs have been eliminated or restructured typically feel unappreciated and undervalued and fear that their current skills and knowledge are no longer sufficient to keep them gainfully employed. While many larger companies provide some form of outplacement services for their white collar workers, those services are seldom enough, and not everyone receives them. Most outplacement services focus on how to conduct a job search and reposition oneself for a new role, but do not provide retraining in the skills those jobs require. Many states have some form of training available for the unemployed, but these programs are rarely adequate and do not address the typical needs of the knowledge worker. If your organization must downsize or restructure for any reason, you can ease the transition for affected employees significantly by assessing their needs and providing both personalized guidance and financial assistance to prepare them for their next position or career move. Even better would be to retrain them for new positions within your own organization, whenever possible.

Although employers typically cease to be concerned with their development needs once employees retire, retirees are another group who may wish to continue to learn and grow. One way to help them while tapping into this valuable resource is to engage them in volunteer work, working with your active employees on community service projects, providing tutoring, training or mentoring to employees and their families, and assisting laid off workers in their transition.

Guidance and feedback

At various times throughout their careers, employees may want or need guidance from a mentor, someone with more experience or a fresh perspective. Whether through a formal program or informal relationships, on-the-job mentoring can ease an employee into a new position or organization and accelerate her progress up the learning curve. Mentoring can also help employees going through a career transition, such as retirement or layoff. A mentor provides an objective and confidential sounding board for the employee's concerns and offers ideas and advice on how to address them, without imposing a specific agenda that the employee must follow.

Frequent positive feedback encourages the employee to continue to perform well, while constructive feedback and coaching can help the employee adjust his approach and improve his performance. Employees often have mixed feelings about receiving feedback, knowing that it can help to improve their performance but also fearing that it may undermine their self-esteem and threaten their sense of security. When feedback is balanced and provided in a non-threatening manner, at the right time and in the right way, employees are more likely to welcome it. Our earlier discussion about respect for the individual bears repeating here. Employees resent being treated as though they need to be fixed, as sometimes happens when managers focus on the gap between individual and ideal skill levels. If instead you acknowledge that everyone has different areas where they excel and encourage employees to select areas where they would like to develop, they are apt to show greater willingness to undertake development plans and to seek assistance in doing so.

Recognition and reward

When incentive compensation is an important part of your employees' pay, they will naturally expect good performance to be appropriately rewarded. But recognition and reward don't end there. Employees want to be acknowledged for their accomplishments and their efforts; when they go above and beyond what's expected of them, they want to be recognized and rewarded accordingly. Recognition may take the form of a direct compliment, sharing the story informally with others, or giving formal recognition in an open forum. A reward doesn't need to be monetary or a promotion; it can be anything that will have meaning to the employee, such as a coveted assignment or time to pursue an area of personal interest. Whenever the accomplishment is the result of collaborative effort, a team celebration is in order.

Another way in which you can recognize employees is by being receptive to their ideas and input, and by acknowledging their contributions, even when their ideas cannot be implemented. Too many rejections can discourage further suggestions, so it is important to acknowledge the positive aspects and explain the reason why something could not be done.

Although traditional status symbols have become less common as corporate hierarchies have flattened, there remains a significant cadre of managers and other professionals who covet the titles and perks that may come with higher level positions. For these employees, power and esteem rank high on their list of personal needs. Older employees want to be recognized for the depth and breadth of their skills and knowledge, while newer employees want to be acknowledged for their technical savvy and fresh ideas.

Employees who are deemed as having high potential for promotion are often put on a fast track and given plum assignments and other perks to keep them engaged. However, while making a select group of employees happy, any of these special considerations may be viewed by other employees as unfair and should be used with caution. Likewise, failure to terminate employees who are not doing their work or who are creating problems has a demoralizing effect on employees who must pick up the slack.

Affiliation

Most employees want to work with others that they like and whose company they enjoy, although the degree of need will vary. While some prefer to work alone, others need the opportunity for frequent interaction with their peers. Most employees are apart from their families throughout the workday; even telecommuters may have limited interactions with their family members during the day. Hence they look to their workplace as an alternative source of human contact.

In the knowledge economy collaboration has become the norm, with employees from different functions coming together to work on a project or process. While these task-oriented interactions are important, people need the chance to interact informally as well and to connect with others beyond their current work assignments. Providing both time and physical space—break room, cafeteria, employee lounge, outdoor seating area, conversation alcoves—for such interactions can have a significant impact on employee morale. In addition, such informal interactions can spawn new ideas that enhance the work and increase job satisfaction.

Another source of employee affiliation comes from belonging to a particular group, whether an outside professional organization or an internal social or special interest group. When employees share interests and participate in extra-curricular activities with colleagues, the bond with your organization often becomes stronger.

3) How they perceive you

Employees perceive you on multiple levels, each of which matters in attracting and retaining motivated workers:

- the organization itself
- management
- their work
- their colleagues

The organization

Employees form their first impressions of you before they are hired. In selecting a potential employer, they look for financial stability and a positive public image. They will seek out firms that have good reputations concerning their policies and practices and that enjoy a level of prestige among their industry peers.

Once they have joined your organization, employees may find their initial impressions reaffirmed or may be surprised to discover that all is not what it seems. Sometimes employees become disillusioned and cynical when they realize that the organization has flaws that belie its external reputation. Alternatively they may find that the organization has hidden strengths that go unrecognized by the general public. They may discover that there is a strong fit between themselves and the internal culture of the organization, or they may realize that they prefer a different working environment. Long after they leave your organization, they may remain loyal customers and shareholders or they may sever all ties, depending on their final assessment of the organization.

Management

It is often said that employees don't leave organizations, they leave managers. While the first part is not entirely true, the second part often is. That is, even when they like their job and the organization they work for, employees sometimes find that they dislike working for a particular manager so much that they are driven to seek employment elsewhere. Conversely, sometimes employees will stay with a job because they like the person they work for, even when they are indifferent to the work or the company itself. Among the crucial factors in how the manager is perceived are her management style, sense of fairness, and overall competence. Employees who respect the ability of their managers and are comfortable with the way in which they are managed tend to be more effective and stay longer in their jobs. These same principles can apply to the overall management as well; employees tend to stay longer and be more productive when they respect and feel comfortable with the way the company is managed.

Middle managers often find themselves serving as mediators between employees and senior management. Some may relish the role, while others may feel caught in the middle, especially in a command-and-control environment. New managers in particular may identify with employees and have difficulty enforcing management policies they may have resisted previously. Enabling your middle managers to help shape those policies can go a long way in resolving those conflicts.

Human resource departments, especially in large companies, are often seen as agents of senior management, setting and enforcing policies that are designed to protect the organization and keep employees in line. They are rarely seen as advocates for employees; yet they are the primary owner of the organization's relationship with employees. Some organizations have created the role of ombudsman to listen to individual employees' concerns and provide guidance; however, this role typically remains outside of the management processes, intentionally so, and hence has limited impact on the overall work environment.

Think about your own organization. Who, if anyone, manages the total employee relationship? What avenues exist for employees to address concerns or provide feedback to decision-makers, without repercussions? How much do senior managers know about employees and their issues? Make note of any gaps and think about how you could address them.

Their work

Earlier we discussed the importance of meaningful work to creating job satisfaction. How employees perceive their job goes beyond the inherent nature of the work itself. Employees may view their work as an important step along their career path or as a source of learning, while volunteers may view it as a good way of giving back to the community. Senior executives may be focused on creating their legacy, not just for the organization but for their chosen field or industry.

Employees may see their work as an essential part of a well-designed process, or they may feel that they are hampered in doing their best work by organizational barriers—structural bottlenecks, ineffective policies, inadequate resources, poor data, and so forth. By identifying and eliminating any barriers, you can not only gain efficiencies but also improve employee morale, leading to even bigger productivity gains.

Their colleagues

How employees view their colleagues is also important. Employees want to work with people who are competent and cooperative. Unfortunately, sometimes organizational policies and practices can get in the way. Traditional planning and budgeting processes sometimes create conflicts within the organization as departments compete for funds and work toward competing goals. Similarly performance appraisals and bonuses based on forced rankings among employees can generate ill will and undermine teamwork among coworkers, potentially resulting in lower productivity and increased employee turnover. The alternative is to assign mutually compatible unit goals aligned with your organizational objectives, design incentive plans and recognition programs that reward teamwork, and foster a culture in which every employee is a partner in serving the organization's customers and managing relationships with your stakeholders.

4) What they can provide/how they impact your business

Employees are a vital part of your value chain, whether they participate in the core business processes that create value for customers, or provide management and support processes to others within the organization. They are also potential customers, shareholders and community members who can have compounding impact on your business. Furthermore, there is strong evidence that employee satisfaction and customer satisfaction are closely linked in a virtuous cycle; happy employees help create happy customers, and vice versa.

It goes without saying that you expect employees to perform their duties diligently and with integrity. You want them to be punctual, dependable, honest and loyal, to respect the confidentiality of the knowledge they have about your organization, to avoid conflicts of interest, and to be good team players. Ideally they will demonstrate commitment to excellence and a willingness to do what's necessary for your customers. But there is still more they can do that adds value.

Volunteer - internal

The simplest way employees can add value is by going above and beyond the scope of their job. This does not mean stepping on someone else's turf, or doing work that is unsanctioned, but simply performing to a higher standard or taking initiative to do more than is required. The employee who volunteers to take on new assignments or raises his hand when no one else will is a godsend to managers with too much to do and not enough time or resources to do it.

Likewise, we cherish those employees who readily extend a hand to their colleagues when they see that someone is overwhelmed. They are often the ones with high emotional intelligence, who know how to bring out the best in others, and who do so without seeking credit for themselves.

Lifelong learning

Another way employees add value is by showing interest beyond their immediate assignment and acquiring a depth of knowledge about the organization. They ask good questions, keep their ear to the ground and regularly scan the environment to understand the competitive landscape and the context in which the business operates. They are quick to understand what is needed and to recognize opportunities when they arise.

Innovation/fresh ideas

The third way of adding value often follows on the second, by generating creative ideas and identifying better ways of doing things. These are the employees who see things differently and are unafraid to challenge the status quo. New hires typically offer a fresh perspective, and veteran employees who are open to change are able to leverage their knowledge and experience to put ideas in motion while avoiding organizational pitfalls.

Problem solving

Similar to the innovators are the problem-solvers. Both bring a level of creativity to their work, but the problem-solvers are typically more structured in their thinking. They are able to analyze a situation or problem, get to the root cause, and formulate a practical solution. While they may have training in Six Sigma or other methodologies, they are more often natural problem solvers who enjoy the challenge.

These are also the employees who are consistently positive contributors, even when they are not formally responsible for finding a solution. They avoid placing blame for a problem and are not afraid to fail, persisting until an answer can be found.

Goodwill ambassador

Employees add value as well through their interactions beyond the organization, by serving as a role model and ambassador to the community and other stakeholders. They may do this through volunteer work or simply through their active participation in community events, such as corporate-sponsored fundraisers or athletic events.

Coaching, mentoring and counsel

Both current employees and alumni can add value by leveraging their knowledge and experience to coach and mentor newer employees. They may serve as a sounding board or offer guidance, career advice, and networking contacts. Subject matter experts may provide education and training in their specific areas of expertise. Seasoned alumni may be invited to serve in an advisory role to senior management on key issues.

Referrals

Employees and alumni can also add value by referring customers and job candidates to the company. Often they have already pre-screened the referral as a good fit and pre-sold the referral on the benefits of a relationship with their organization. As a result, the cost of acquiring that customer or recruiting that candidate is typically lower than average, and the retention is apt to be greater as well.

5) How you can enhance your relationships

Employee retention, especially of your most valuable employees, is crucial to the long term health and success of your business. Not only is it cost-effective as a means to protect your investment in talent development, but also it contributes to greater customer loyalty and therefore higher sales. Retention is not the same as commitment, however, and commitment is a two-way street.

Consider what you have learned about your employees, and identify possible ways to enhance your relationships. Think also about potential hires and alumni, each of whom can enhance your business through goodwill. Do not limit yourself to the suggestions below.

Senior management connection

Many employees in large or hierarchical organizations sometimes feel as though senior management is unaware of their existence. You can boost morale by ensuring that senior managers make time to meet with new employees to learn about their talents and interests and to make them feel welcome; then meet with each employee periodically to acknowledge their contributions and to see how they are doing. Doing this regularly helps management check the pulse of the business while gaining a deeper appreciation for the talent within your organization.

Enrich the work environment

As you assessed the wants and needs of employees, you no doubt uncovered gaps that could be addressed to improve employee satisfaction. In addition to satisfying fundamental needs such as competitive compensation packages and benefits and a safe, comfortable work environment, the best organizations provide a healthy, supportive work climate in which employees can thrive and grow. To create such an environment, you may adopt policies and practices such as the following:

- Eliminate distractions and reduce unhealthy stress by communicating openly with employees and involving them in decisions about issues that matter to them, providing flexibility to enable them to balance their work and personal lives, and making each person feel valued and secure;

- Staff adequately to avoid burnout and to provide bench strength; ensure sufficient capacity to allow for training and development, special assignments and both planned and unplanned absences; encourage employees who are ill to take time off to recover;

- Provide opportunities for employees to utilize their skills and special talents beyond their specific jobs; encourage them to participate on special projects or committees, internal or industry and professional special interest groups, and volunteer programs;

- Recognize people for who they are and what they contribute to the diversity of talent and experience; celebrate achievements and encourage and support individual development efforts through active listening, coaching, mentoring and peer partnering;

- Provide opportunities within your business for cross-training and career progression; enable employees to shadow someone in another department, rotate people through different functional areas or roles; establish an exchange program with an outside partner;

- Encourage employees to speak their minds freely, without fear of criticism or retribution; listen closely and welcome their concerns, ideas and insights; give them opportunities to implement their ideas; encourage thoughtful risk-taking and help them learn from their mistakes;

- Provide occasions for social interaction, enabling candidates, employees and alumni to form or renew personal relationships that strengthen their ties to your organization.

Foster entrepreneurial innovation

For most organizations, providing the sort of enriched environment described above is challenging enough. Nonetheless, true trailblazers may choose to take the suggestions a rather daring step further, by giving employees the time and space to fulfill their own entrepreneurial visions. Rather than have talented people leave the organization to strike out on their own, they are given permission to work on projects they care about within your existing work environment. Whether or not they retain some of their responsibilities, they are given time to pursue their vision, along with the shared services and resources typical of a business incubator. In exchange, your organization typically has the right of first refusal to share in the success of the initiative, in whatever way makes sense given the particular circumstances.

In the remainder of this chapter, we provide an overview of the two remaining operational stakeholder groups—suppliers and distributors—and other key stakeholder groups. You are encouraged to explore these groups in depth, noting who your stakeholders are in detail, what they need from you, how they perceive you, how they impact you, and how you can enhance your relationships with them.

I-C: Suppliers

The typical supply chain originates with the extraction of natural resources and ends with the purchase of a finished product or service by the consumer. Where you sit and the nature of your business determines who is a supplier, a distributor or a customer. Suppliers are upstream, providing inputs to your organization, while distributors are downstream, taking your outputs—perhaps transforming them—and getting them into the hands of your ultimate customers.

Generic Manufacturing Supply Chain

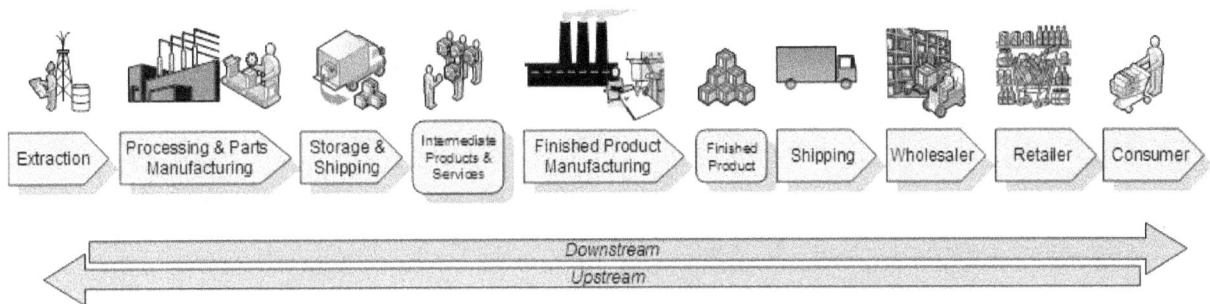

Sometimes the same stakeholder can be both a supplier and a customer. Take for instance a recycling company. The community and the commercial establishments and residents within its boundaries are the company's customers who receive waste management services. At the same time, the brokers who buy the recycled materials and the companies that reuse them are also customers of the recycling company. From this latter perspective, the communities that provide the waste products to be sold are upstream suppliers.

Volumes have been written about supply chain management, and your organization may already be using state-of-the-art methods for your most important suppliers. Nonetheless, it behooves you to review your understanding of those suppliers and their concerns, as well as the smaller, less crucial suppliers who may interact on a transactional basis with only a few buying units within your organization.

Again, it is up to you to decide what level of analysis is relevant and useful to your organization. You may want to consider such characteristics as size and scope of relationship, nature of products and services purchased, suppliers' financial strength, and other risk factors. You will need to consider upstream suppliers, as well as distinct roles within each supplier, such as sales and operations. Once you have identified your supplier stakeholders, you may assess what they want and expect from you, how they perceive you and your organization, and what value they can provide to you and you to them.

Who's Who?

An example of overlapping supplier-distributor-customer roles is the complexity of multiple flows that occur among investors, financial firms and homebuyers in the residential mortgage business, as illustrated below. While investors provide the funds that the bank ultimately lends to the homebuyer, the bank in turn provides the mortgage loan for inclusion in a mortgage pool that backs securities that offer a range of risk-return investment choices for the investor. The principal and interest payments made by the homeowners provide multiple streams of payments that provide a return to the investors. The bank originating the mortgage loan is a supplier to both the homeowner and to the firm securitizing the assets.

Sample Financial Supply Chain – Home Mortgage

A. Funding Flow

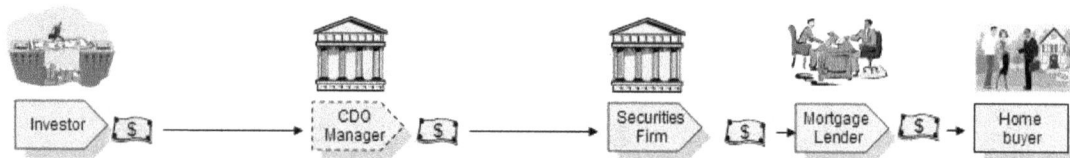

B. Securitization flow

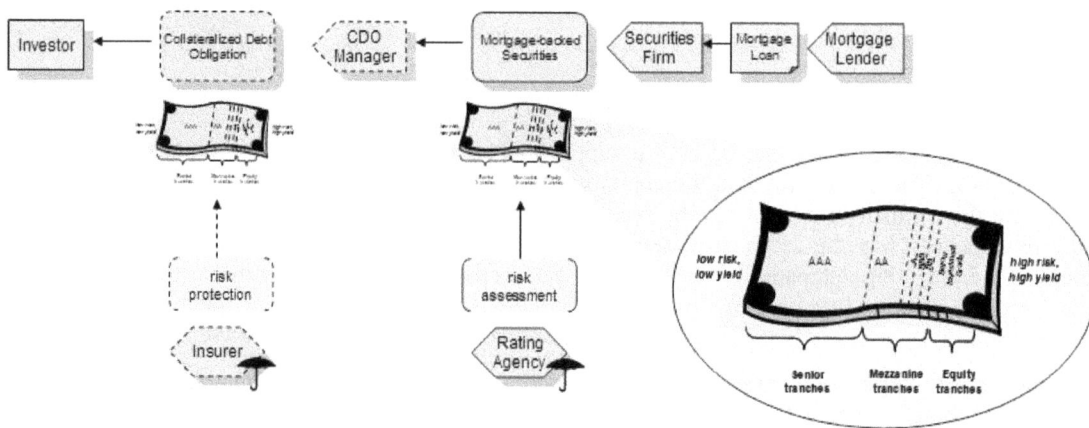

C. Payment flows

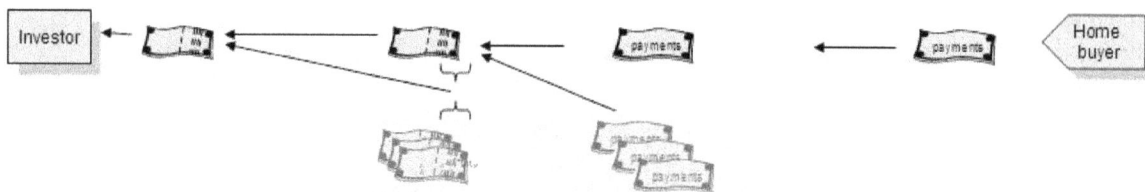

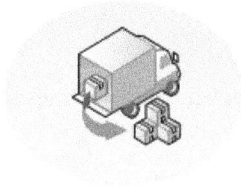

I-D: Distributors and ancillary services

Distributors are those who are downstream from you and whose ultimate purpose is to get products and services into the hands of customers as efficiently as possible. Your distribution system depends upon the nature of your products and the concentration of your market, among other factors. Distribution channels may range from single layer, such as direct mail or online, to as many as five layers, involving retailers, wholesalers, and manufacturing agents or jobbers.

Each of these layers may be further segmented—retail into franchisees, consignees, independents and department stores, for instance—and each distributor may be one of many or have exclusive distribution rights within a given region or market. They may distribute your products and services exclusively, or provide a range of competing products and services. A distributor may be a value-added reseller, packaging products or services from others together or providing additional services themselves, or a broker of commodity products and services. Each distributor may provide a variety of functions, including physical possession and transportation, advertising and promotion, order taking and payment processing, financing and customer service.

In addition to the distributors themselves, you may want to consider businesses that provide customized ancillary support to your distribution network, such as logistics, transportation, storage, insurance, trade financing and advertising. For those distributors who handle competing products and services, you may need to consider who those competitors are and your relative share of the channel. When you have identified the players in your distribution network, you can then think about their needs and impact on your business.

II. Strategic Stakeholders

Strategic stakeholders are organizations who operate in parallel to your own and whose businesses are synergistic with yours. They include those with whom you have formed a direct relationship, as well as arms-length relationships with organizations whose products and services are often bought or used together with yours, such as hardware and software or air travel and car rentals.

II-A: Business partners and alliances

A strategic alliance is a direct collaborative relationship between you and one or more independent organizations, typically undertaken to share expenses and resources, reduce risk and pursue a common objective, such as joint marketing, research or co-production. Each of you contributes your own unique strengths to the endeavor, including such resources as products, customer referrals, distribution channels, manufacturing capability, project funding, capital equipment, knowledge, expertise, or intellectual property.

There are various types of strategic alliances, including joint ventures and other equity-based partnerships, non-equity contractual relationships, and informal business referral arrangements, each of which has its own structure and obligations. You may form strategic alliances that reach across national and industry boundaries, joining forces with a wide variety of organizations, including suppliers, customers, competitors, universities, NGOs and government units. Every alliance is unique in what your partners want and expect from you, how they perceive you, and the value each party brings to the relationship.

II-B: Franchisors/franchisees

Unlike strategic alliances, in which partners are typically on equal footing, the franchisor holds the balance of power over its franchisees. If you are the franchisor, you make the rules and enforce the standards. Your newest franchisees may depend on you for guidance in managing their business, while your more established franchisees may seek more influence and a loosening of the reins. You may be the sponsor of a franchise advisory council, or your franchisees may have formed their own organization exclusive of you. You may work with area developers who own multiple franchise units, including those of your competitors.

Similarly, if you are a franchisee, your relationship with the franchisor will be a function of the degree of maturity of your business, the presence of company-run units, and the potential involvement of an area developer. In addition, you may have relationships, both informal and through a formal organization, with fellow franchisees.

Whichever your role, consider the individual and collective needs, expectations and perceptions of the other parties, as well as your own, as they evolve over time. Look for opportunities to increase the value you both provide to and receive from these relationships.

II-C: Complementary enterprises

Although lacking the formalized relationship of a strategic alliance, complementary enterprises are strategically important to you as well, and you to them. These are the organizations whose products and services are often paired with yours and whose fortunes are therefore linked with yours. The linkage may be merely associative—as between air travel and car rentals, burgers and fries, snow shovels and ice melt, baseballs and bats, houses and homeowners insurance—or technical—as between electronic hardware and software, printers and ink cartridges, lamps and light bulbs, hybrid cars and refueling stations, tax forms and tax filing programs. In the first case, the products and services are often, though not necessarily, bought or used together by the consumer and enhance each other's value to the customer. In the second case, the products must be compatible, conforming to agreed-upon standards, in order to function properly.

Think about those businesses which are potentially complementary to yours, now and in the future. They may include non-profits, universities and government agencies, as well as for-profit companies. Consider how well aligned you are today and what changes may be ahead. Then assess your relationship with each enterprise and look for ways to enhance the linkages you share, including coordination of marketing and setting of standards.

III. Financial Stakeholders

Financial stakeholders are those that many businesses often think of first and foremost. While they include shareholders, they also include private owners, creditors, donors and others who provide financial support to your business, whether in the form of debt, equity, lease financing, grants, endowments or gifts, as well as guarantees, credit ratings and secondary markets.

Governments may provide financial support to your business through subsidies, loans, guarantees and other programs. To the extent that their role is broader and more policy-driven, they may also be considered in the Business Environment category. Include them wherever you feel is most relevant to your business.

III-A: Shareholders, owners and investors

Your business may be a parent company or a wholly owned subsidiary, it may be publicly traded or privately owned, and it may have few or many owners or investors. Investors may include large institutional investors, such as retirement funds, mutual funds, investment trusts, banks and insurance companies, as well as venture capitalists and both large and small individual stockholders. Individual investors may be active day traders or they may be long term investors, perhaps indirectly through mutual or retirement funds.

Your common stockholders may be represented by a Board of Directors, comprising both internal and external directors, with various ties to other organizations as well as yours. Your Board may also have nominating, compensation, audit, finance, and executive committees to carry out specific functions, and may have strong or weak ties to management or to certain investors. In addition to common stockholders, who are equity owners, you may have preferred stockholders, who are passive investors.

If your business is closely held, as are 90% of all U.S. businesses, perhaps yours is a family-owned business, with close ties to the founders. You may receive private funding from an angel investor or venture capital firm, through direct equity investments, loans, or other financial arrangements. If you are preparing to go public with an IPO, you may be underwritten by an investment bank or syndicate, or may raise capital through an online trading house.

The financial objectives of your owners and investors may be short term or long term, and may include capital growth, tax shelter, dividends, or underwriting fees. Their investment in your business may be a small part of a much larger portfolio, or it may represent their life's work. As you think about your equity stakeholders and their representatives, consider what needs and expectations they may have beyond the return on their investment, such as fulfilling a personal mission or acquiring a position of power and prestige.

III-B: Trustees, sponsors, donors and contributors

If your organization is a nonprofit enterprise, you typically have a Board of Trustees instead of a Board of Directors. Although they don't have the same relationship with donors as a for-profit Board of Directors has with shareholders, one of the main responsibilities of your non-profit board members is to ensure financial accountability of the organization. Board members act as trustees of your organization's assets and must exercise due diligence to ensure that they are used to support your organization's mission.

Your non-profit's financial resources may come from a wide range of sources: government agencies, charitable foundations and trusts, corporations, venture capitalists, estates, philanthropists, subscribers and other individual donors. Your organization may be the named beneficiary of a donor's life insurance policy or retirement plan, and the recipient of funds in the form of grants, endowments, major gifts, charitable gift annuities, planned giving, annual donations, sponsorships, cause-related marketing, pro bono services and in-kind donations, fundraising pledges, subscription fees and one-time donations.

Funds may be directed to a specific purpose or may be unrestricted, allowing your organization to use the funds as you see fit to support ongoing programs, general operations or strategic growth. Increasingly, donors are looking for assurance that their gifts have significant impact, including an emerging class of growth investors with different expectations from their more traditional counterparts.

Besides donors themselves, a number of intermediaries have emerged to assist would-be donors by providing insights and guidance in selecting worthy recipients. One such organization familiar to individual donors is Charity Navigator, an independent charity evaluator of the financial health, accountability and transparency of America's largest charities. Another is the Bridgespan group, whose philanthropy website (www.GiveSmart.org) offers a "Donor Decision Tool", among other materials to enhance the effectiveness of philanthropic giving. More recently, two former hedge fund analysts have established GiveWell, a nonprofit that applies their expertise to evaluate charities with hedge-fund-level rigor. Because they may have considerable impact on your nonprofit's perceived attractiveness to would-be donors, it behooves you to assess such intermediaries as stakeholders as well.

III-C: Creditors

A major source of funding for your business may come from various creditors, such as bondholders, commercial banks, trade creditors, finance companies, government agencies, private individuals and, in the case of financing leases, equipment lessors.

Each of these creditors may hold a unique position in the hierarchy, depending on the nature of their lending relationship with your business, such as whether the debt is secured or unsecured, senior or subordinated, investment grade or below, and so forth. Should your business be close to bankruptcy, even customers may turn out to be creditors, albeit unintentionally, when they have prepaid for a purchase or bought a gift card for your retail business.

III-D: Financial guarantors and third parties

Besides those who actually provide funds, you may also have others who provide guarantees, letters of credit or insurance to protect you or your creditors from financial losses. In addition, complex financial products have created a whole new class of financial stakeholders who may have an interest in your business. Those stakeholders may include such third parties as credit rating agencies, investment analysts, financial counterparties and intermediaries, trustees, upstream investors of securitized obligations, and short sellers, to name but a few. It behooves you to understand who these parties are and the extent to which their interests are aligned with, or against, your own.

IV. Business Environment Stakeholders

The next group of stakeholders plays a major role in creating the business environment in which you operate. Collectively they make the rules, set the standards, promote certain interests, and otherwise work to influence the competitive landscape. The extent to which their interests align with yours determines whether they act as enablers or barriers to your business. Understanding and responding to the legitimate interests of all parties, and leveraging the collective power of like-minded individuals and organizations, can create a more favorable business climate.

IV-A: Government and regulators

Governments and their agencies—local, regional, national or international—play a major role in shaping the business environment through such means as policies, laws and regulations, judicial proceedings, taxes and tariffs, subsidies, permits and public services. Each level of government in turn may include executive, legislative and judicial branches, each playing a distinct role which may vary widely from one jurisdiction to the next.

Government programs, policies and regulations may be specific to your industry or sector, such as banking regulations, farm subsidies or small business loans, or may be general—environmental regulations, for instance, or privacy laws—and apply to all businesses. Their purpose may be supportive or restrictive toward your business, or simply intended to ensure a level playing field— e.g., export financing, insurance regulations and antitrust laws respectively. Government services that affect your business include such diverse categories as infrastructure, public health and safety, law and order, water and sanitation, and emergency management.

The governmental organizations that affect your business are influenced in turn by outside parties, such as lobbyists, political activists, and local commissions and ad hoc committees. As you assess the crucial stakeholders in this category, consider also who these external influencers may be and what impact they may have on your business.

IV-B: Professional, trade and industry associations

You or your employees may belong to one or more professional, trade or industry organizations whose goal is to promote the interests of its membership. These organizations serve various functions on behalf of their membership, such as public relations, setting standards, educating members, monitoring regulations and lobbying government. Professional associations may also oversee certification and licensing, effectively controlling the supply of licensed practitioners.

An association in which you are a member may be local, regional, national or international, or may be a local chapter of a federal organization, such as the U.S. Chamber of Commerce. Membership may be at the corporate level, covering all your active employees, or it may be individual, limiting benefits to those who have paid dues.

Through active participation in these associations, your business may exert a level of influence you would be unable to have on your own. In addition to its own activities, an association may form, or contribute to, a political action committee to promote certain issues that affect your business.

IV-C: Labor unions

Depending on the nature of your business, your stakeholders may include one or more labor unions. Even if your workers are not unionized, unions may influence the wage levels, benefits and other working conditions prevalent in the marketplace, including those for middle managers and others outside of the unions' purview.

Traditionally, labor unions followed the industrial model, based on adversarial relationships with employers and demanding uniform standards and treatment of workers, who were presumed to be interchangeable. Newer, "reform" labor unions, on the other hand, abolish traditional principles in favor of collaboration, flexibility, role differentiation and greater discretion at the local level. In either case, the union seeks to bargain collectively on behalf of its members and to ensure their protection from abusive or discriminatory practices.

It is not sufficient, however, to assume that the interests expressed by union officials are always identical to interests shared by all of their members or your employees as a whole. It is prudent to look beyond the official union demands to fully understand the needs and concerns of their members, as well as those of non-union employees.

IV-D: Competitors

When most of us think of competitors, we think of those who compete for a share of customers' wallets. However, your business competes not just for customers, but also for talent, scarce resources, suppliers, funding, and distribution channels, among other economic factors. Furthermore, competitive advantage among customers is not based solely on the merits of your products and services, but may also depend on such attributes as your ability to measure your environmental impact or to meet just-in-time demand.

To complicate matters further, organizations can be both your competitors and your allies at the same time. For instance, they may be complementors in making a market—for high definition televisions, for example, or by forming a food court within a shopping mall—but become competitors in dividing the market. Similarly, companies may cluster together to capitalize on easy access to resources, such as skilled labor pool or business incubator services, and then compete for that talent or office space.

Consider your competition in this broader framework and identify those who have significant current or potential impact on your business. Identify what drives them and look for areas where you can derive mutual benefit.

V. Public Interest Stakeholders

The last group of stakeholders is perhaps the most diverse and wide-reaching, ranging from private citizens and special interest groups to society as a whole and Planet Earth itself. These stakeholders, while not your primary focus, are often affected by your business and may affect your business in turn. As many organizations have discovered, should you ignore them, you do so at your peril. To be recognized as a good corporate citizen, you must look after the legitimate concerns of your public interest stakeholders.

V-A: Communities

Although the particular details will differ from one community to the next, local residents and organizations alike are concerned about the quality of life and working conditions within their community. To ensure that your presence is welcome within the community, you need to understand and address their concerns. The more you understand and respect the local history, institutions and culture, the greater your acceptance is likely to be.

At a minimum, you are expected to avoid doing harm—e.g., displacement of local businesses, increased burden on local infrastructure, potential health and safety issues, or other unwelcome disruptions to the status quo. Beyond that, your business demonstrates good citizenship by sponsoring programs that improve the quality of life in the community. In addition to providing financial support to existing community events and programs, consider launching new initiatives that address unmet needs within the community and that connect to the community on a personal level.

In addition to getting to know elected and appointed officials, identify other members of the community who bring different perspectives, such as educators and members of local civic groups. Consider the best ways to engage them and incorporate their views into your decision making. Recognize how they view themselves in relation to the broader community and the world, and adapt your interactions accordingly.

V-B: Environment

Planet Earth has long been the silent stakeholder of most businesses, but that is rapidly changing, with global climate change and increased scarcity of vital resources at the forefront. Not only is Planet Earth affected by your business, through your consumption of resources and your impact on natural processes, but also it affects your business in turn, through its ability to provide essential resources and a hospitable environment in which to operate.

To fully understand this unique stakeholder, you need to consider it from multiple aspects. The issues you most likely recognize focus on the quality of air, water and soil, along with the greenhouse effect and depletion of non-renewable energy sources. Other concerns include the loss of biodiversity among the earth's flora and fauna, resulting from disruption of migratory paths, destruction of habitats, interruption of the natural food chain and interference in natural processes of growth and renewal – all unintended consequences of human activity.

Even when an activity itself seems benign, such as fishing, the cumulative effect when too many perform the same activity can be devastating. Alternative energy sources used by your business today may reach a tipping point some day in the future, when too many wind turbines and solar panels have changed the air currents, altered weather patterns, or reduced the heat available for plants. The proliferation of electronic signals from smart phones, tablets and other devices we all use to manage our businesses and personal lives may one day disrupt communications necessary for the reproductive success of certain species, such as bees and other pollinators, which in turn affects the ability to grow crops. CFLs may improve energy consumption of our homes and businesses but eventually the accumulated mercury will have its own deleterious impact.

Think about the impact your business has on the environment. Consider how you can replace non-renewable resources with recycled or renewable ones, reduce or replace toxic chemicals, and optimize the energy and water used throughout your product's lifecycle. Look for ways to reduce any waste in your packaging, improve the efficiency of transportation of supplies and finished goods, and employ green practices for design, construction and maintenance of your facilities.

V-C: Society

Increasingly, companies are recognizing the potential impact their business decisions have on society as a whole, and vice versa. The larger and more global your business, the greater the likely impact on society, whether in terms of quality of life, health and safety, economic wellbeing, civil rights or other societal issues.

The impacts of your business decisions may be positive, negative or both, and may be compounded whenever business practices are adopted widely across an industry or region. Downsizings, plant closings and mortgage foreclosures may affect entire communities, even regional or national economies, while new technologies—think internal combustion engines of the past and smart phones of today, for example—may transform the way society functions. Decisions to source from third world countries may foster growth of a middle class yet raise questions about human rights, labor practices and political freedom, while solutions developed for the bottom of the economic pyramid—low cost drugs or water filters, for instance—may help alleviate disease and raise the standard of living for millions of people.

Think about the ways, intentional or otherwise, in which your business impacts society as a whole. Consider not just your own actions but practices common to your industry, and assess the likely impact, both short term and long term, on society. Look for ways your business can protect the public good and enhance the quality of life for the greatest number of people.

V-D: Special interest groups, non-profits/NGOs and educational institutions

The interests of many other organizations beyond those already mentioned may intersect with yours, whether positively or negatively. Among these are non-profit organizations and NGOs (non-governmental organizations) that perform a variety of service and humanitarian functions; educational institutions at all levels, including related alumni associations; political groups, including Super-PACs, political parties and lobbyists, and other special interest groups, such as religious organizations, hobbyists and civic groups.

Non-profits and NGOs often have considerable influence in national or world affairs, impacting the social, economic and political activities of communities and governments. They and other special interest groups may either applaud or denounce your humanitarian, environmental or other policies and either seek to thwart you or partner with you to advance your common interests. Educational institutions may supply the talent and skills needed to conduct your business, through suitable course offerings and internships.

Think about those groups whose interests align or are in opposition with yours. Look for and reinforce areas of mutual agreement while seeking to mitigate any differences. Pay particular attention to correcting any misperceptions they may have about your business. Consider how you might partner with those groups whose interests align with yours to further advance your cause.

V-E: Media, general public, bloggers

The world of media is going through a digital transformation so rapid that this section—both content and format—may well be out of date by the time it is published. This transformation has magnified its potential influence on your business, for better or worse. The public has greater and more instantaneous access to information than ever before. Technologically savvy shoppers can compare prices via their smart phones and use that information to demand a discount or take their business elsewhere.

Today very little that you do escapes notice and any story about you, whether true or false, has the potential to go viral. With ready access to social networking tools, a single individual can ignite a firestorm over your activities or policies—as happened to Bank of America when the bank attempted to impose fees for debit card usage—or launch a viral marketing campaign or instigate a "cash mob"—causing a sudden surge in sales for a particular product or store. Indeed, widespread communications helped foster recent political upheaval in the Middle East and the localized "Occupy" movement across the United States.

Think about the various trade publications and news media that may impact your business, whether via print, broadcast, cable, internet, or other digital channels. Get to know the reporters and bloggers who are apt to latch onto stories about you, your competitors or other important stakeholders and make sure they have a good understanding of your business. While you cannot control what others may publish, you can control your response by monitoring what's being said and preparing a well-considered reply, as appropriate.

Assessing strategic possibilities

As you have been analyzing your stakeholders, you have identified various gaps in your relationships or discovered ways in which you might enhance those relationships by providing more value and receiving more value in return. If you have not already done so, now is a good time to pull all of those ideas together in preparation for the next phase.

Focusing on those stakeholders with whom you want to develop stronger relationships, summarize the current status and the strategic possibilities you have identified for each. You may wish to summarize your analysis using a stakeholder assessment worksheet, such as shown on the following page. (Columns have been compressed to allow the sample to fit on a single page width. Your own worksheet will need to be wider to accommodate meaningful commentary.)

An example of a partially completed worksheet, using an alternative format, is shown below.

Stakeholder *(may be either a group or individual)*	Relationship Status (and Target)					Strategic Possibilities *(close gaps, eliminate barriers, provide/receive additional value)*	
	Extremely negative	Somewhat negative	Mixed, neutral or unknown	Somewhat positive	Extremely positive		
Foreign distributors	☐	☐	S	☐	→T	Provide bilingual marketing materials	
Overseas customers	☐	☐	S	☐	→T	Provide bilingual instructions	
Overseas prospects	☐	☐	S	→T	☐	Provide bilingual marketing materials	
Foreign competitors	☐	S	→T	☐	☐	Adopt common standards	
Foreign government	☐	☐	S	→T	☐	Keep well informed about plans	
International partner	☐	☐	☐	☐	S	Assist in obtaining US visa	
Etc.	☐	☐	☐	☐	☐		
	☐	☐	☐	☐	☐		

Stakeholder Assessment Summary Worksheet

Stakeholder/Role (may be either a group or individual)	What they want	What they can provide	Relationship: Status (from) Target (to)	Gaps/ barriers/ issues	Strategic Possibilities*	Ease (H/M/L)	Impact (H/M/L)

Relationship Status/Target:

1. Extremely negative
2. Somewhat negative
3. Mixed, neutral, or unknown
4. Somewhat positive
5. Extremely positive

*ideas to improve understanding, close gaps, eliminate barriers, provide/receive additional value

Assigning relationship oversight

As you reviewed your relationships with your stakeholders, you were asked to consider how those relationships are being managed and by whom. While every employee is responsible for treating stakeholders with respect, it behooves you to assign one or more persons to oversee the policies and practices for interacting with each group of stakeholders.

Some relationship management roles may already exist within your organization, e.g., the heads of marketing/sales, purchasing, human resources, finance, public affairs, corporate social responsibility, investor relations, legal, and so forth. However, the nature of their role as relationship leaders may differ somewhat from their traditional roles, which tend to take a more protective stance, placing the organization's self-interest above all others. For instance, the human resources department in many organizations has become less of an ally to employees and more of an enforcer of management policy; sometimes the only advocate for employees is one person with limited influence acting as ombudsman.

Adopting a value-driven strategy places greater responsibility on these traditional positions for establishing guidelines and processes to enhance those relationships and for coordinating with one another to align policies and balance conflicting stakeholder interests when they arise. Depending on the structure of your organization, you may choose to leave the traditional roles alone and establish new positions to take on the relationship role. Either way, formalizing the coordination among the relationship leaders is most effective in ensuring a consistent, value-driven approach. This group or their designees may form the core team for the remaining exercises in this book.

Stakeholder Relationship Assignment Worksheet

Stakeholder group	Relationship Leader (Name and/or Title)	New position?

Exercise 2: Stakeholder Network/Community

During the Stakeholder Analysis you considered each of your stakeholder groups individually and identified possible ways to enhance those relationships. The next analysis goes a step further, looking at the relationships among your stakeholders and identifying ways to make them mutually beneficial.

You begin by identifying existing relationships or influence between and among your stakeholders. Do your suppliers have direct relationships with your customers or competitors? Do your customers have influence on government regulators or local communities where you operate? Do your business partners have access to different markets that represent desirable prospects for your business? Do any of your partners or employees have close ties with academic institutions where vital research is being conducted?

Consider both positive and negative relationships among your stakeholders and assess their relative strength. Are there adversarial relationships between your suppliers or distributors and certain public interest groups? Is the media critical of your partners or your industry? How entrenched are these relationships, and do they help or harm your own relationships?

Also consider whether these relationships are unilateral, bilateral or multilateral, i.e., involving three or more stakeholders simultaneously. For instance, a local community may have influence over its state representative (but not vice versa, hence unilateral), while a competitor may belong to an integrated supply chain that includes one or more of your suppliers and distributors.

As you consider these relationships, recall what you learned about how different stakeholders perceive you. Are they aligned in their views, or do they see you quite differently? Which stakeholders are more closely aligned with how you see your own organization? What might cause these differences, e.g., do stakeholders differ in their core values and objectives, or might they have insufficient or inaccurate information about your organization? How might these differences be addressed?

Stakeholder Network Worksheet

Key Stakeholder	Relationship(s)	Direction (1 = unilateral, 2 = bilateral, 3 = multilateral)	Status and strength (check one):					Impact: + helpful - harmful (blank = neutral)	Shared view (High, Medium, Low, Blank if unknown)
			Strong negative	Negative	Weak	Positive	Strong positive		
			☐	☐	☐	☐	☐		
			☐	☐	☐	☐	☐		
			☐	☐	☐	☐	☐		
			☐	☐	☐	☐	☐		
			☐	☐	☐	☐	☐		
			☐	☐	☐	☐	☐		
			☐	☐	☐	☐	☐		
			☐	☐	☐	☐	☐		
			☐	☐	☐	☐	☐		
			☐	☐	☐	☐	☐		
			☐	☐	☐	☐	☐		
			☐	☐	☐	☐	☐		
			☐	☐	☐	☐	☐		
			☐	☐	☐	☐	☐		
			☐	☐	☐	☐	☐		
			☐	☐	☐	☐	☐		
			☐	☐	☐	☐	☐		
			☐	☐	☐	☐	☐		

The collective pattern of relationships among your stakeholders forms a network like the simplified example depicted in the diagram below.

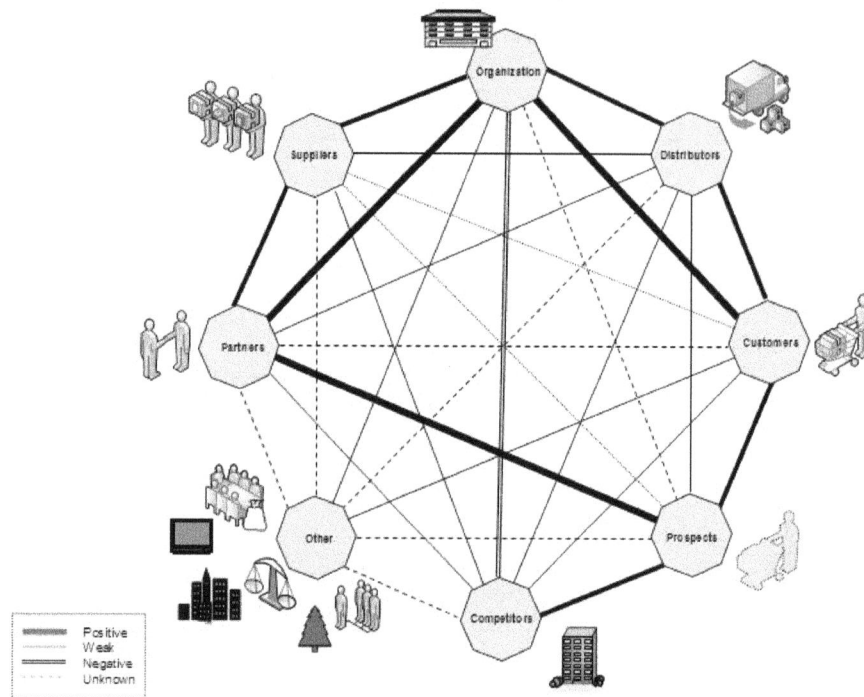

Note that, in the diagram, your organization appears as one node among equals, rather than the center of a hub; this view enables you to focus more clearly on relationships that exist beyond your own organization. Each node may be a single category, such as customers, or sub-category, such as prospects, or it may represent a single important stakeholder, such as a key supplier or competitor. Your network will have many nodes and linkages; select the ones that have the most potential, for either help or harm, and focus your analysis on those inter-relationships.

The following is a simple example of an organization whose international partner provides access to overseas markets and advocates with the foreign government on behalf of the organization. In return, the organization may assist the partner by leveraging its own relationships with domestic suppliers.

Sample company network worksheet:

Key Stakeholder	Relationship(s)	Direction (1 = unilateral, 2 = bilateral, 3 = multilateral)	Status and strength					Impact: + helpful - harmful (blank = neutral)	Shared view (High, Medium, Low, Blank if unknown)
			Strong negative	Negative	Weak	Positive	Strong positive		
International partner	Domestic suppliers	2	☐	☐	X	☐	☐		Low
	Foreign distributors	2	☐	☐	☐	☐	X	+	Medium
	Overseas customers	2	☐	☐	☐	X	☐	+	Low
	Overseas prospects	2	☐	☐	X	☐	☐	+	Low
	Foreign competitors	2	☐	X	☐	☐	☐		Low
	Foreign government	1	☐	☐	☐	X	☐	+	Medium
Foreign competitors	Foreign distributors	2	☐	☐	☐	X	☐	-	
	Overseas customers	2	☐	☐	☐	X	☐	-	
	Overseas prospects	2	☐	☐	X	☐	☐	-	
	Foreign government	unknown	☐	☐	☐	☐	☐		
Foreign distributors	Overseas customers	2	☐	☐	☐	☐	X	+	
	Overseas prospects	2	☐	☐	☐	X	☐	+	
	Foreign government	unknown	☐	☐	☐	☐	☐		
Overseas customers	Overseas prospects		☐	☐	☐	X	☐	+	High
			☐	☐	☐	☐	☐		

The interrelationships in this example are depicted in the following diagram.

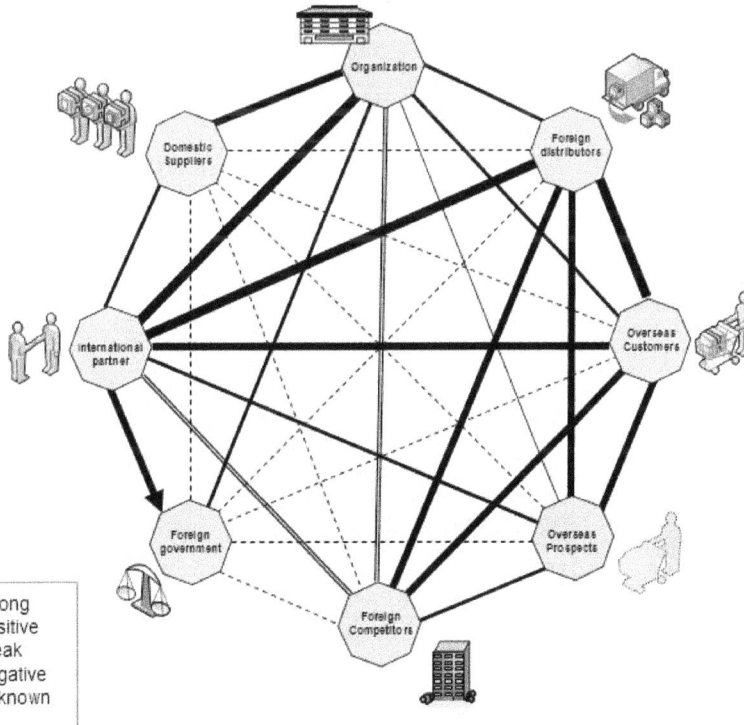

From network to community

The next step in the analysis is to consider ways in which to strengthen your network, by leveraging relationships and increasing the congruence among stakeholders' perspectives. For instance, you may enlist a supplier with influence in your local community to make introductions and lend support to your local initiative. Likewise, you may form an advisory panel comprising customers, suppliers and distributors to assist you in identifying and opening up new markets. Similarly, you may educate your industry group, local governments and special interest groups about the safety or environmental impact of your processes, thereby allaying their concerns and gaining their mutual support for a new initiative. Even adversarial relationships with stakeholders such as competitors can be drawn closer through deeper understanding and alignment around industry standards and similar business issues.

One of the most common ways of strengthening a network is to bring together key suppliers and distributors to align and streamline processes through a supply chain management system. Similarly, design charrettes that bring together customers, employees, communities, suppliers, environmental groups and other stakeholders are increasingly used to increase alignment before undertaking a new development project.

As your stakeholders become more aligned and relationships become multi-lateral, the network is transformed into a mutually beneficial stakeholder community. As you build your community, you increase your reservoir of business capital, i.e., the resources and capabilities at your disposal. (For a detailed explanation of business capital, see Exercise 3.)

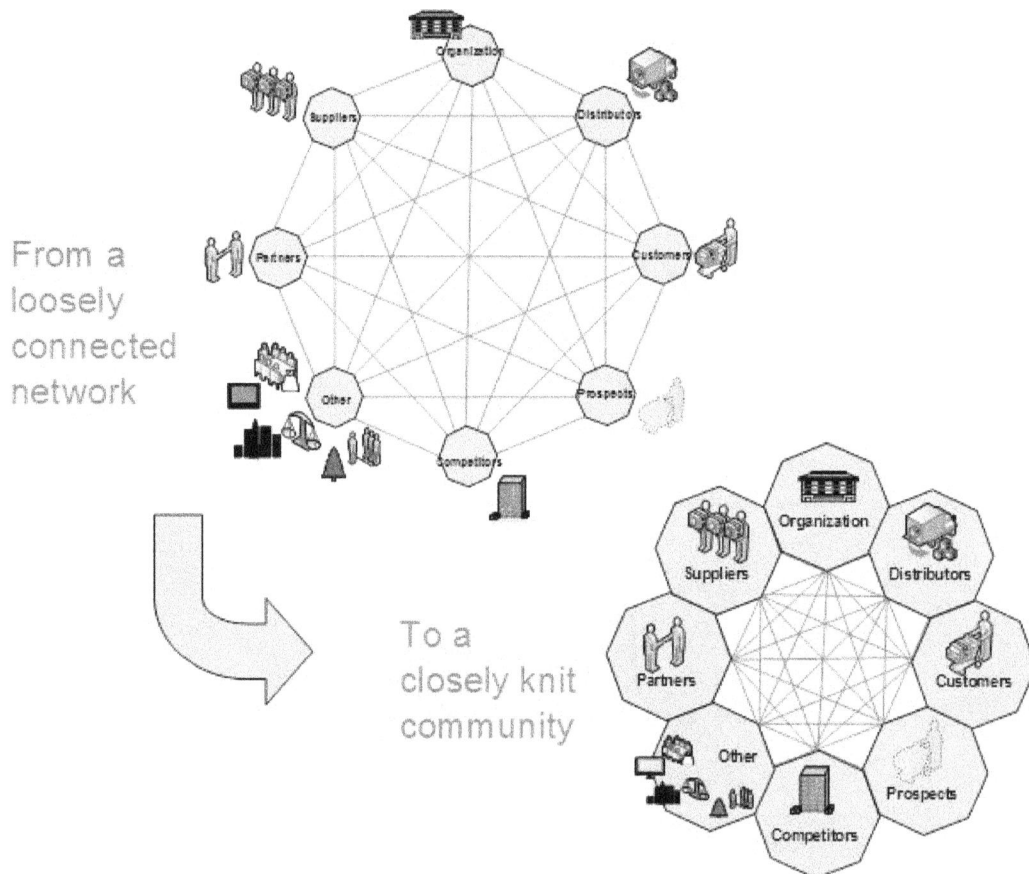

From a loosely connected network

To a closely knit community

Revisit your list of possibilities identified during the Stakeholder Analysis and add new ideas that will help strengthen your network and build a community with a shared understanding and sense of purpose. Also identify any new stakeholders you wish to add, such as local communities, NGOs or select media, to round out your stakeholder community.

In our previous example, the organization seeks to leverage the overseas relationships of its international partner to strengthen its own relationships. The organization establishes a target for improving each relationship, including those that are candidates for membership in its stakeholder community, and identifies possible actions it might take, as shown below.

Stakeholder *(may be either a group or individual)*	Relationship Status and Target					Strategic Possibilities *(original stakeholder relationship ideas from Exercise 1, plus additional ideas to strengthen network)*	Potential community member (Y/N)
	Extremely negative (adversary)	Somewhat negative	Mixed, neutral or unknown	Somewhat positive	Extremely positive (advocate)		
Foreign distributors	☐	☐	S	☐	→T	Provide bilingual marketing materials **Hold trade conference**	Y
Overseas customers	☐	☐	S	☐	→T	Provide bilingual instructions **Create custom website for registered customers** Hold user conference	Y
Overseas prospects	☐	☐	S	→T	☐	Provide bilingual marketing materials **Hold user conference**	Y
Foreign competitors	☐	S	→T	☐	☐	Adopt common standards	N
Foreign government	☐	☐	S	→T	☐	Keep well informed about plans	N

In most cases, it is unrealistic to expect that every stakeholder will become part of your stakeholder community. More likely, the majority will remain outside of the central community, along a relationship continuum ranging from positive to middling to negative, with the most negative, adversarial relationships on the outermost ring. While your primary efforts may focus on the innermost circle, do not ignore the rest of your network. Ideally you want to draw every stakeholder closer; at a minimum you need to consider policies to protect your social capital, preserving the goodwill of your more positive stakeholders while addressing the concerns of the most negative. (For an explanation of social capital, see Exercise 3.)

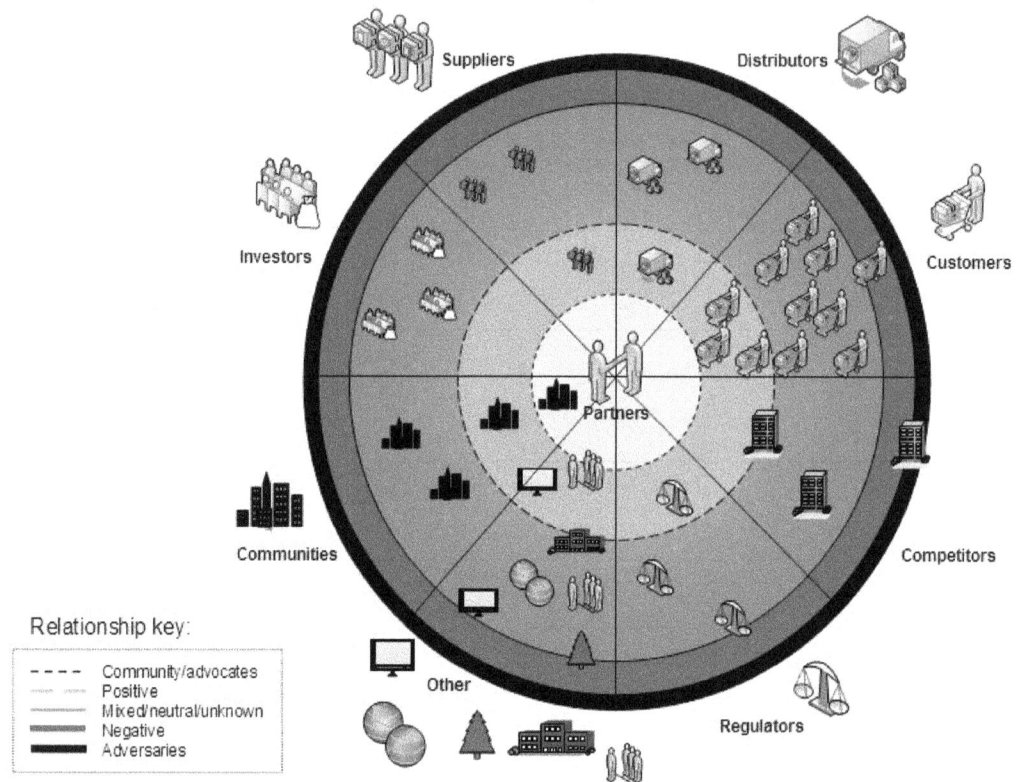

Relationship key:

- - - - Community/advocates
——— Positive
——— Mixed/neutral/unknown
——— Negative
■■■ Adversaries

Stakeholder (may be either a group or individual)	Relationship Status and Target					Strategic Possibilities (original stakeholder relationship ideas from Exercise 1, plus additional ideas to strengthen network)	Potential community member (Y/N)
	Extremely negative (adversary)	Somewhat negative	Mixed, neutral or unknown	Somewhat positive	Extremely positive (advocate)		
Adversaries	S	☐	→T	☐	☐	Seek to neutralize	N
Somewhat negative	☐	S	→T	☐	☐	Seek to neutralize	N
Unknown	☐	☐	S	☐	☐	Ascertain status	N
Mixed	☐	☐	S	→T	☐	Address their concerns	N
Neutral	☐	☐	S	→T	☐	Keep well informed about plans; gather insights and seek ways to add value	N

Exercise 3: Business Capital Inventory

At any point in time your organization has a diverse set of resources and capabilities upon which to draw. Some of these are tangible assets, such as your facilities and bank accounts, while others are intangible, such as your reputation and relationships. Collectively they provide your organization what we shall refer to as your business capital, the lifeblood of your organization and the means by which you are sustained.

Business capital is the accumulated value derived from your own organization and your stakeholders, as well as the external environment. You can either build up or erode your capital base through your actions and attitudes, and through engagement with your stakeholders. In addition, normal wear and tear and the passage of time can erode your capital, and external factors can either enhance or diminish your capital.

Types of capital

We have identified the following nine types of business capital[4]:

- Social
- Human
- Intellectual
- Market
- Financial
- Organizational
- Physical
- Environmental
- Civic

Let us take a look at each type of capital, where it comes from, why it's important, and how you can—intentionally or unintentionally—generate more or deplete your supply. As we go, take stock of your organization's own capital and the rate and means by which you are accumulating or using up the capital you have currently.

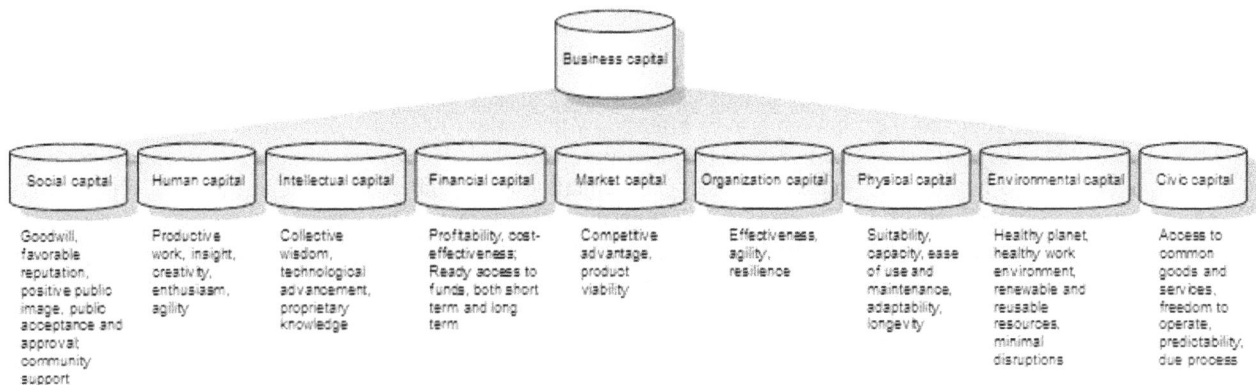

Social capital	Human capital	Intellectual capital	Financial capital	Market capital	Organization capital	Physical capital	Environmental capital	Civic capital
Goodwill, favorable reputation, positive public image, public acceptance and approval; community support	Productive work, insight, creativity, enthusiasm, agility	Collective wisdom, technological advancement, proprietary knowledge	Profitability, cost-effectiveness; Ready access to funds, both short term and long term	Competitive advantage, product viability	Effectiveness, agility, resilience	Suitability, capacity, ease of use and maintenance, adaptability, longevity	Healthy planet, healthy work environment, renewable and reusable resources, minimal disruptions	Access to common goods and services, freedom to operate, predictability, due process

---

[4] Terms as used here may differ somewhat from their definitions in other contexts.

Social capital

Perhaps the most ephemeral business capital your organization can have is social capital. Social capital typically comprises such elements as a favorable reputation and positive public image, the goodwill and trust generated with each of your stakeholders, broad-based public acceptance and approval, and strong stakeholder support and advocacy. Social capital is a fundamental component of a value-driven strategy and is derived largely from your organization's ethics, values, attitudes and behaviors, and the value you exchange with each of your stakeholders. Your social capital can also be impacted by matters over which you have little direct control, such as public mood or perceptions of the industry, home country, or other category to which your organization belongs.

An adequate reservoir of social capital acts like a lubricant for your business, helping to keep the wheels of progress turning smoothly. Without adequate social capital, you are apt to find each undertaking an uphill battle, with one obstacle after another standing in your way, until stakeholders are confident that their interests are being protected. Once enough social capital has been established, stakeholders feel more comfortable and less guarded, and things begin to go more smoothly, with fewer challenges to overcome.

Social capital is enhanced whenever you behave with integrity, place others' interests ahead of your own and take a proactive stance in resolving problems that arise, without defensiveness or casting blame. You cultivate social capital by demonstrating ethical behavior, transparency, accountability and sensitivity to others' concerns throughout your organization. You offer quality products and services at a fair price, treat people with respect, are honest in your dealings and seek win-win solutions with your stakeholders. When a problem occurs, you act swiftly to resolve it, placing the safety and well-being of others ahead of your own concerns, keeping them informed and mitigating the negative impacts on their lives. When problems arise that cast a shadow over your industry, you take a leadership role in correcting them and putting measures in place to prevent their recurrence.

On the other hand, social capital can be eroded by providing poor quality products and services or engaging in unfair, predatory or deceptive practices. Secrecy, defensiveness, and lack of sincerity can further undermine your social capital. If you appear unwilling to take responsibility, preoccupied with your own welfare, or slow to react to a negative situation when it arises, your stakeholders will take note and withhold their support. Social capital, once lost, can be difficult to recapture.

Your social capital can also be affected by the actions of your stakeholders and by external factors beyond your control. For instance, inappropriate behavior by an employee or unethical policies of a key supplier can undermine your capital. When your industry or business in general comes under attack for perceived excesses or abuses, your own social capital is diminished.

Human capital

It has become a management cliché, especially within the knowledge industry, to remark that a company's assets walk out the door every night. The observation is meant to acknowledge the importance of employees to the successful functioning of the business. But is it really true? And does management treat employees as valued assets, or do those words ring hollow?

As an employer, you don't own your employees and, unless there's an employment or labor contract in place, you have no legal claim on an employee's future services. What you do have is a talent pool from which to draw and the willingness of employees to show up again tomorrow and to apply their knowledge and skills productively on behalf of your organization. This is your human capital.

Human capital comprises ready access to a workforce with the skills, knowledge and abilities needed to run your business, in combination with the productive efforts, insights, and creativity of your employees and their willingness and enthusiasm to continue contributing their talents to the work of the organization. It is derived from the individual and collective abilities, knowledge, skills, attitudes and behaviors of employees in conjunction with a supportive work environment and effective leadership. Having adequate human capital is essential to running your business; maintaining and growing your human capital is essential to sustaining your business in the long run. Without adequate human capital you are constantly running in place, as turnover and low productivity constrain your progress.

Human capital begins with attracting and retaining talented people with the necessary skills, knowledge and abilities and whose values are aligned with those of your organization. It is further enhanced by inspiring them to do their best work, treating them fairly and with respect, and providing an environment in which they can flourish. You cultivate human capital when you communicate openly and honestly, demonstrate sensitivity to work-life balance issues, and provide training and development opportunities to those who desire them. You partner with local communities and educational institutions to attract or develop an educated workforce. You preserve human capital in difficult times by finding alternatives to downsizing and by protecting the rank and file employees first and foremost.

Human capital is diminished by engaging in unfair labor practices, placing unreasonable demands on employees, and fostering a hostile work environment. Anything you do, intentionally or otherwise, that distracts employees from the work to be done or undermines morale erodes your human capital. A performance management system that feels punitive rather than helpful, a cookie cutter approach that leaves no room for individuality or creativity, policies that prevent people from taking care of vital personal matters during the workday, and admonitions to do more with less or to "work smarter, not harder" without providing the time and resources to redesign the work—all serve to diminish your human capital. When you treat employees as though they were consumables to be used up rather than as assets (albeit leased, not owned) to be preserved and maintained, you erode your base of human capital.

Your human capital can also be affected by your stakeholders and matters beyond your control. For instance, work stoppages, injuries or defection of key players can reduce your human capital. Changing demographics can either shrink or expand the available talent pool over time, likewise altering your human capital.

Intellectual capital

Your intellectual capital comprises the collective wisdom and expertise within your organization, including whatever technologies and proprietary knowledge you may possess and on which your business depends. It is derived from your organization's knowledge base, along with the means to capture, analyze and utilize that knowledge to manage the business.

Although it may resemble human capital in some instances, for the most part they are not the same. When a typical employee whom you have trained leaves the organization, you lose a bit of human capital momentarily but regain it when you hire and train their replacement. However, when that employee had specialized know-how that is vital to the business, you lose some of your intellectual capital as well, which is harder to replace. That is especially true if no one else in your organization has that same know-how. Intellectual capital is often the primary and most obvious source of your competitive advantage.

You build intellectual capital by creating a learning organization, gathering pertinent information and mining the data for useful insights, and institutionalizing the knowledge throughout the organization. You systematically scan the internal and external environments and seek feedback from your stakeholders. You foster systems thinking and creativity among your employees and you refresh your intellectual capital by bringing in new perspectives and ideas, while stimulating new insights among seasoned employees. You protect your proprietary knowledge while exchanging ideas with customers, professional and industry associations, and educational institutions, as well as suppliers, distributors and other stakeholders. When appropriate, you license technology to or from your stakeholders.

You squander intellectual capital by failing to capture the specialized know-how and institutional memory embodied in the subject matter experts and veteran workers within your organization and among your stakeholders. Myopic thinking, internal focus and inadequate analysis can prevent you from developing your intellectual capital to its full potential. Finally, intellectual capital may have a limited shelf life; hence, failure to keep up with new developments and technologies can quickly erode your intellectual capital base.

As with other forms of capital, your intellectual capital can be affected by your stakeholders and other external factors outside of your control. Technological breakthroughs may render your own technology obsolete, or industrial spying and copyright infringement may deplete your capital base. On the other hand, expiration of a competitor's patent may open up new opportunities, enhancing your intellectual capital.

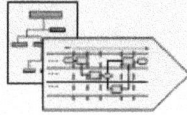

Organizational capital

Your organizational capital may be the most unrecognized, undervalued resource of your organization. Organizational capital comprises the overall effectiveness, agility and resilience of your organization, and is an outgrowth of your structures and systems, policies and practices, and processes and relationships. The amount of organizational capital you have determines how successful you are in executing, how readily you are able to respond to changes, and how capable you are of enduring prolonged downturns in business.

Organizational capital is enhanced when you streamline processes and decision-making, foster meaningful and lasting relationships with stakeholders, and develop sufficient bench strength and contingency plans to cover unforeseen circumstances that may arise. You conscientiously monitor progress and eliminate roadblocks, involve employees and other stakeholders in making continuous improvements, and ensure that everyone is on the same page.

Organizational capital can be undermined by bureaucracy, outdated or uncontrolled processes, and cumbersome policies and decision-making. Lack of accountability, inconsistency and failure to follow through can further weaken organizational capital. You risk losing organizational capital during a merger, downsizing or other major restructuring unless steps are taken to quickly realign the organization into a single, cohesive unit with clear focus and adequate resources.

Market capital

Your market capital is the competitive advantage of your products and services taken collectively, including market share and speed to market. It is derived from your brand; the quality, affordability and availability of your products; their pricing and positioning; and their unique combination of features that satisfy important customer needs.

Market capital is enhanced by having quality products and services and by pricing and positioning them appropriately. You strengthen your market capital when you maintain a strong and favorable brand, offer a mix of products at various stages of the product lifecycle, and have a robust research and development process that enables you to quickly recognize and respond to new market opportunities. Market capital is further enhanced by having sufficient scale and scope to achieve a cost advantage, and by controlling channels of distribution.

Market capital is diminished by lackluster products and services, weak demand, erratic supply, inappropriate pricing or positioning, an imbalanced mix of products across lifecycle, declining market or market share, weak or negative brand image, and a lengthy or undisciplined product development process.

Market capital is influenced by external changes as well, such as new entrants to or departures from the marketplace, aggressive tactics by a competitor, technological advances, supply shortages, demographic shifts and changes in consumer tastes.

Financial capital

Financial capital, as we define it here, is more than just what appears on the balance sheet. Financial capital means having ready access to funds, both short term and long term, and the wherewithal to generate or obtain as much as needed without onerous terms and conditions. Financial capital encompasses your borrowing capacity and creditworthiness, your profitability or cost-effectiveness, and your attractiveness as an investment. Without adequate financial capital, you are unable to take advantage of opportunities when they arise or to weather a major economic downturn.

Financial capital is enhanced by demonstrating financial discipline, investment savvy and the ability to generate revenues and manage costs consistently. You strengthen your financial capital when you honor your financial commitments, live within your means and make prudent investment decisions based on a thorough assessment of risks, costs and benefits. You further protect your financial capital by offering attractive, quality products and services at a fair price and on fair terms, ensuring financial accountability and transparency, and enforcing a rigorous set of financial controls.

Financial capital is eroded by shoddy recordkeeping, a lack of discipline and accountability, inadequate planning, short term focus, and an absence of controls. Most crucially, failure to accurately assess and mitigate risks can quickly destroy your financial capital.

Externally your financial capital is affected by economic conditions, such as economic stability, inflation, resource availability and cost, tax laws, trade agreements, and available subsidies.

Physical capital

The physical capital of your organization goes beyond the tangible assets themselves—such as land, buildings, equipment and materials—to include the suitability, capacity, ease of use and maintenance, adaptability and longevity of those assets. Hence, two assets that appear to perform the same essential function may represent different levels of capital, depending on their design.

For instance, one equipment model may be limited to a single purpose or a small (inadequate) volume, while another can handle a greater volume or may be modified and adapted to another purpose; hence the latter possesses the greater capital. Alternatively, the first may be made of flimsy material, resulting in a shorter useful life, or be fragile and costly to maintain, while the second may be durable, easy to maintain and long-lasting, thereby increasing its capital over the first. Lastly, one asset may be complex and difficult to use properly, requiring significant investment in training, while the other may perform just as well but be easy to use with minimal training. Unless an asset is needed only temporarily or for limited usage, the greater the capacity, ease of maintenance, adaptability and useful life, the more physical capital is generated, enabling your business to run more smoothly and to respond more quickly to changing needs.

Physical capital is enhanced whenever you make smart purchasing decisions—including make-buy-or-lease and selection of the specific model, ensure proper operation and maintenance, and provide adequate training to all users and maintenance staff. Physical capital is eroded whenever you acquire unsuitable equipment, allow unqualified personnel to operate the equipment, use it incorrectly or for an unintended purpose, or fail to provide adequate maintenance and a clean, orderly work environment.

Outside of your control, vandalism or theft can reduce your physical capital, as can severe weather or natural disasters such as earthquakes, wildfires and landslides.

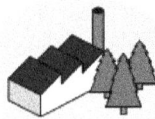

Environmental capital

Increasingly business is coming to recognize the value of environmental capital and to take steps to protect it. Environmental capital comprises a healthy environment for your stakeholders, including a healthy planet and its ability to provide an ongoing supply of clean, renewable and reusable resources. It encompasses all of our natural resources—such as air, water, earth, sunlight, energy, flora and fauna—and the biological systems that support them and the natural processes that replenish them. Your environmental capital is derived from your policies and processes, consumption of resources and waste management practices, and is essential to the well-being of your organization and your stakeholders. Because our planet's natural resources are shared by all, environmental capital can also be affected by the policies and actions of others, including your own stakeholders and other organizations.

Your environmental capital is enhanced whenever you take measures to protect and conserve natural resources. Locating your work facilities near public transit, encouraging telecommuting and minimizing the impact of employee travel and transportation of goods all help reduce energy costs and emissions, thereby increasing your environmental capital. Developing eco-friendly products, reducing packaging and taking back products at the end of their useful life to reuse component materials further enhance your capital. Other common measures to enhance environmental capital include improving energy efficiency, preventing pollution and erosion, reducing water usage, increasing reliance on natural light, and using non-toxic, renewable or recycled materials.

Environmental capital is eroded whenever you use natural resources irresponsibly, generate waste, and destroy natural habitat and migratory routes of important species. You lose environmental capital when you cut down mature, healthy trees, pave large swaths of land, and locate your workplace in a location that is accessible only by car. It is lessened still further when your construction and demolition debris ends up in a landfill, your operations create noise pollution or electro-magnetic disturbances, or you leave lights on and computers running when there's no one there. And unfortunately, your environmental capital is eroded even if you do none of these things, but others do.

Civic capital

As with environmental capital, civic capital is largely rooted in the external environment. It represents your access to public goods and services, freedom to operate, and due process through a system of law and order. It is derived from the infrastructure, public services, laws and regulations, and the legal system. Civic capital provides a level playing field and enables your business to operate both locally and globally in a predictable manner in accordance with a set of established rules.

Your civic capital is enhanced through your responsible use of the public infrastructure, systems and services, contribution to the tax base through corporate and personal taxes, and compliance with existing laws and regulations. You increase civic capital when you clean the sidewalks in front of your establishment, conduct fire drills and develop emergency evacuation plans.

Civic capital is eroded whenever you abuse infrastructure or public services, evade taxes, skirt laws and regulations, or abuse the legal system. Whenever you use vehicles that exceed the size or weight limits of roads and bridges, blast air conditioners with the doors open during hot summer days, and dump snow in the street or in the local water supply, you are eroding civic capital. Likewise, when you file frivolous lawsuits, seek undue political influence, or jeopardize public safety, you undermine civic capital.

Unsurprisingly, civic capital can also be eroded or enhanced by factors beyond your control, such as aging infrastructure and acts of terrorism, as well as the carelessness and abusiveness of others.

Sources of business capital

Internal strengths and weaknesses

As described above, business capital can come from, or be depleted by, several different sources over which you have varying levels of control. First and foremost, your capital is derived from your internal **strengths**, such as your positive leadership and efficient organizational structures, and diminished by your internal **weaknesses**, such as undisciplined processes and outdated technology.

Stakeholder benefits and detriments

Second and equally important, it comes from your stakeholders, often in response to the value you provide to them. Sometimes it will be explicit, as in the form of public recognition or information sharing. More often it will be implicit, as in the enthusiasm with which workers do their jobs or the reliability of suppliers. As with internal sources, it can be either positive, enhancing your capital base, or negative, diminishing it. We might call these **benefits** and **detriments** respectively, to distinguish them from your internal strengths and weaknesses. You influence these sources through your engagement with stakeholders, but you do not have direct control.

Exogenous advantages and disadvantages

Lastly, business capital can come from factors beyond your sphere of influence, such as conditions in the external macro environment which may affect other firms, as well as internal factors unique to your organization but over which you have no or very limited control. Examples from the external environment include the global economy and state-of-the-art technology, while internal examples include the health and well-being of employees. Again these may be positive or negative, which we will call **advantages** and **disadvantages**, to distinguish them from the previous sources.

Think about your own sources and drains of business capital and identify ways in which you can protect and build your capital. We will revisit these sources when we discuss the Expanded SWOT Analysis in the next chapter.

Current Sources of Business Capital

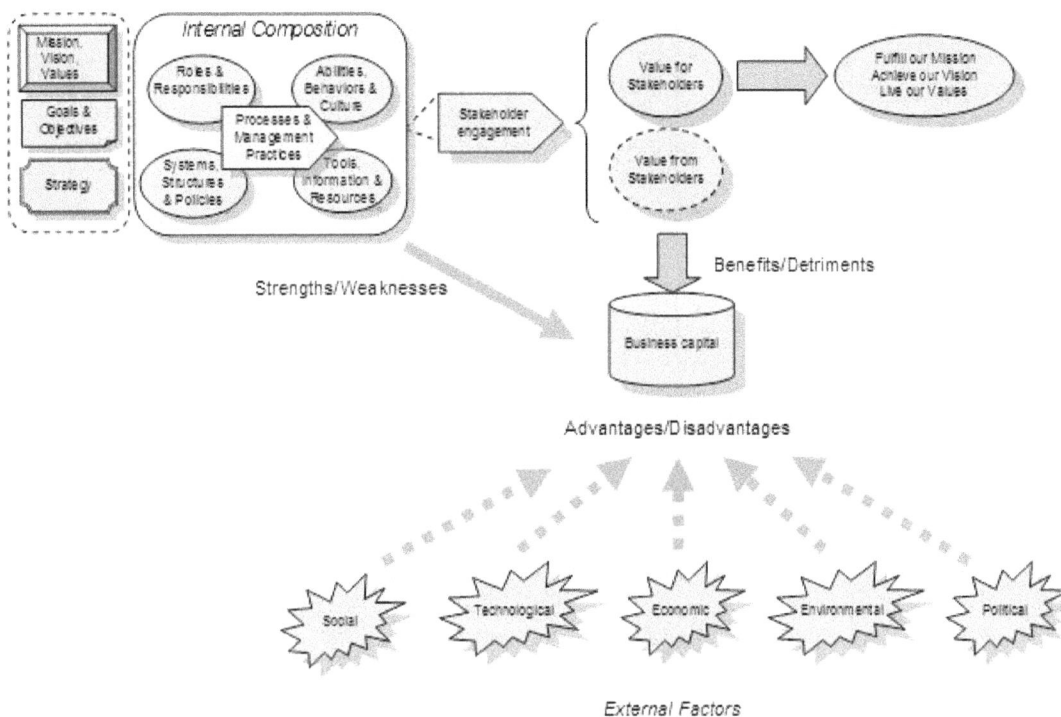

Business Capital Inventory Worksheet

Business Capital:	Sources:					
	Internal/Within Our Control		From Our Stakeholders		Exeogenous/Beyond Our Control	
	Strengths (+)	Weaknesses (-)	Benefits (+)	Detriments (-)	Advantages (+)	Disadvantages (-)
Social						
Human						
Intellectual						
Organizational						
Market						
Financial						
Physical						
Environmental						
Civic						

Exercise 4: Expanded SWOT Analysis

Traditional SWOT Analysis with which you may be familiar typically looks at only two sources of capital over time—internal strengths and weaknesses that exist today, and opportunities and threats from the external environment that may occur in the future. Our Expanded SWOT Analysis takes a more granular approach, looking at each of the three of the sources mentioned in the previous exercise—internal levers within your control, your stakeholders, and external factors beyond your control—in both timeframes, present and future. These different perspectives are depicted, along with examples, in the simple matrix below.

We have already described the sources in the left half of the matrix, representing the current sources of your business capital. You will want to leverage or capitalize upon those that are positive, while you will seek to eliminate, minimize or mitigate those that are negative. The right half looks at future possibilities arising from the same sources. These are not merely the actions taken in response to the current situation, but represent new situations arising from growing trends, changes in circumstances and possible events that may occur in the future. These situations may affect your future business capital; hence you need to anticipate and prepare for their possibility.

Expanded SWOT Matrix

	Present		Future	
	+	-	+	-
Within Our Control	Strength e.g., economies of scale	Weakness e.g., product defects	Potential e.g., R&D breakthrough	Risk e.g., loss of focus
From Stakeholders	Benefit e.g., licensed technology	Detriment e.g., buyer defaults	Booster e.g., fast ramp up	Buster e.g., manager misconduct
Beyond Our Control	Advantage e.g., healthy staff	Disadvantage e.g., recession	Opportunity e.g., Mideast peace	Threat e.g., natural disaster

Internal potentials and risks

First consider those internal sources of business capital that will be largely within your control if and when they occur. For instance, you may have an R&D breakthrough that significantly improves your competitive position, enhancing both your intellectual and market capital. You need to be ready to capitalize on that potential. Alternatively, over time the organization may slip into complacency, losing focus and weakening your organizational capital in the process. You need to take steps to guard against this possibility and the risk it poses to your organization. Hence we refer to such positive and negative future sources of capital as **potentials** and **risks** respectively.

Stakeholder boosters and busters

Stakeholders may also present new sources or destroyers of business capital. For instance, a supplier who can quickly ramp up production should there be a sudden surge in demand provides a boost to your organizational and market capital, while a manager found guilty of sexual harassment can undermine your social capital. We refer to these positive and negative sources from stakeholders as **boosters** and **busters** respectively.

External opportunities and threats

Finally, the external environment can provide a wide range of future possibilities that can enhance or erode your business capital. These are the **opportunities** and **threats** of the traditional SWOT Analysis, and they come in five basic flavors: social, political, economic, technological and environmental. Many of these, such as demographic trends or a change in political party control, can be difficult to classify in advance as positive or negative, as they depend on your organization's unique situation. For instance, a long, hot, dry summer may be devastating to farmers but a boon to manufacturers of air conditioning units. A list of sample factors is provided in Exhibit 3.

Future Sources of Business Capital

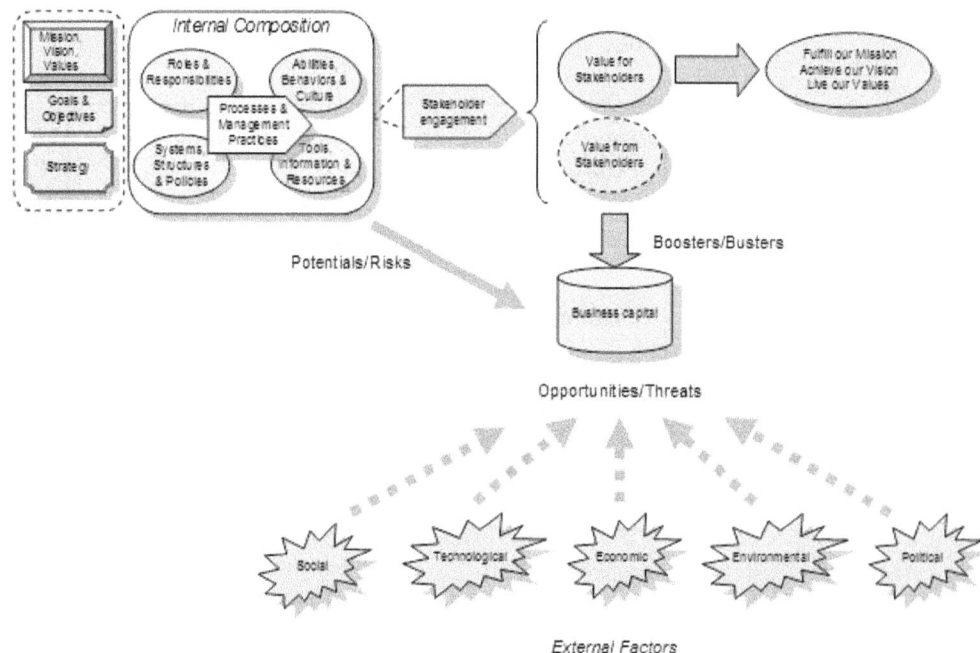

Exhibit 3: Examples of External Factors

SOCIAL

Urbanization
Literacy/ education
Population size
Demographics
Employment patterns
Labor movements
Life styles
Family structure
Minorities/women
Language/culture
Crime
Healthcare
Religion
Immigration
Privacy issues

ECONOMIC

Recession
Inflation
Energy costs
Labor costs
Taxes
Unemployment
Resource availability and costs
Distribution of wealth
Business cycles
Reliability of forecast
Accounting practices
Degree of integration (vertical vs. horizontal)
Free markets vs. planned economies
Conservation policies
Social security reform

ENVIRONMENTAL

Climate change
Extreme weather events, e.g.:
- hurricanes
- tornados
- lightening strikes
- avalanches
- wildfires
- floods
- droughts

Geologic events, e.g.:
- volcanic eruptions
- earthquakes
- tsunamis
- landslides

Astronomical events, e.g.:
- solar flares
- meteor strikes
- asteroids

Electromagnetic radiation
Habitat loss
Species extinctions
Invasive species
Infestations
Soil erosion
Deforestation
Air quality
Water quality
Ozone levels

POLITICAL

Nationalism/regionalism
Protectionism
Populism
International conflict
Terrorism
Multinationals
Cartels
Laws and regulations
Political climate
Home country prestige abroad

TECHNOLOGICAL

Communications
Information technology
Personal computing
Methodologies
Distribution
Transportation
Energy
Satellite
Aeronautics
Electronics

In addition to the macro conditions that affect most other organizations along with yours, there may be factors beyond your control that affect a much smaller subset of organizations, such as an increase in local air traffic or the expiration of a competitor's patent. Finally, there are factors beyond your control that affect your organization alone, such as worker health issues or nearby construction.

Thinking ahead

Because the possible future sources can be quite numerous, with widely different implications for your organization, you need a simple way to identify and prioritize them. Begin by brainstorming the many possible internal developments and external trends, changes and events that could impact your organization. Is your employee base getting older, moving from household formation and family toward empty nests and retirement? Are your suppliers at risk of being acquired by the competition? Could public services, such as the US postal service, be eliminated or significantly reduced? Might the corporate tax code or government subsidies be changed substantially?

As you think about each possibility, consider its potential impact and the implications for your business. Think about the likelihood of occurrence, the importance and timing of each situation, and any interdependencies or combinations that could compound the impact. Do some possibilities preclude others? Are there likely scenarios where several possibilities occur at the same time?

Prioritize your responses based on the likelihood, urgency, ease of responding and degree of impact, assigning top priority to those important situations most likely to occur soonest or requiring significant lead time. Less urgent situations may allow a staged response or, for those unlikely scenarios requiring minimal lead times, you may be able to defer your response and monitor for any changes. Assign the lowest priority to those possibilities that are both extremely unlikely and largely inconsequential.

It is strongly recommended that you prepare contingency plans for those situations that are unlikely but nonetheless crucial should they occur, such as natural disasters or terrorism. History has shown that highly improbable events do occur, often with tragic consequences. The 2011 earthquake and tsunami that decimated Japan's nuclear plant is but one recent example.

Response Matrix

		Importance		
		Low	Moderate	High
Likelihood	High	Minimal preparation	High priority	Top priority
	Moderate	No action	Moderate priority	High priority
	Low	No action	Contingency plan	Contingency plan

Illustrative example

A hypothetical example of possible developments and their impact is shown in the following table. Note the potential synergies among the responses. Relocating operations and distribution closer to urban centers but away from vulnerable areas also reduces the distance for transporting goods. Building backup power supply reduces the negative impact of disruptions in the power grid from both manmade and natural causes. Putting contingency plans in place for ramping up for new products or sales growth may also help protect the organization from the impact of multiple staff defections.

Sample Analysis of Future Events:

		TREND/ POSSIBLE CHANGE OR EVENT	BUSINESS IMPLICATIONS/ SOLUTIONS	CAPITAL AFFECTED	DEGREE OF IMPACT					
					How likely? (1 = low, 5 = high)	How important? (1 = low, 5 = high)	Overall impact	Potential (+) or Risk (-)	Timeframe	Ease (Low to High)
INTERNAL COMPONENT										
	Technology	R&D breakthrough	Ramp up to introduce new product line	Intellectual Market Organizational	4	5	20	+	M/T	L
	Facilities	Obsolescence of equipment	Need to replace or upgrade	Physical	4	4	16	-	L/T	H
STAKEHOLDER										
	Customers	Significant sales growth	Need to ramp up operations and customer service	Market Organizational	3	5	15	+	M/T	M
	Employees	Critical mass of staff defections	Cross-train backup teams and/or establish outsourcing alternative	Human Intellectual	3	4	12	-	S/T	M
EXTERNAL FACTOR										
SOCIAL	Demographics	Increased concentration of population in urban centers	Relocate distribution centers closer to cities	Market Organizational	5	3	15	+	L/T	L
POLITICAL	Homeland security	Threat of hacking into power grid by terrorists	Ensure backup power for critical operations	Civic Organizational	3	5	15	-	S/T	M
ECONOMIC	Oil prices	Upward price pressure	Reduce reliance on gas-fueled transportation	Financial Organizational Physical Environmental	4	5	20	-	S/T	M
TECHNO-LOGICAL	Robotics	Increased automation of warehouse logistics	Potential to move to 24/7 operation	Organizational Human	3	3	9	+	M/T	L
ENVIRON-MENTAL	Climate change	Increased disruption by extreme weather events	Relocate operations from vulnerable areas	Organizational Environmental	4	4	16	-	S/T	L

Part II: Strategy Formulation

In the previous step, you assessed the status of your stakeholder relationships and reservoir of business capital, and identified possible ways to enhance both. The next step in planning is to decide where you want to go and what path you will take. What are you trying to accomplish, and what is the best way to do it? How will you know when you get there and whether you are making progress?

In this section we introduce four new analytical exercises that can help your organization address these questions and establish clear strategic focus by concentrating on your organization's strategic drivers:

- **Exercise 5: Mission, Values, and Rules of Engagement**
  An in depth analysis of your organization's purpose and the fundamental principles and beliefs that guide your actions

- **Exercise 6: Envisioning the Future**
  A brainstorming exercise to define a compelling future state for your stakeholders to which you aspire

- **Exercise 7: Strategy Mapping**
  A thorough analysis of the objectives and the critical success factors that will get you to your vision

- **Exercise 8: Strategic Scorecard**
  The translation of your strategy into measurable goals and milestones to monitor your progress

Exercise 5: Mission, Values and Rules of Engagement

Your organization's mission and enduring values form the foundational underpinnings of your business. Together they define what you stand for as an organization. As such, they typically remain fairly stable over time and are subject to change only under extraordinary circumstances, such as radical transformation of an industry or market. Your mission and values are primary sources of social capital and key drivers of your value-driven strategy.

Whether you are defining your mission and values for the first time or rethinking the existing ones, it is important to ensure that it is a group effort, led by a core team and affirmed by the larger organization. Ideally the core team will include leaders at multiple levels across the organization, individuals who represent the different viewpoints that exist both inside and outside the organization. The initial focus is on identifying the key concepts, words and phrases that are most meaningful to you as an organization. Once everyone on the core team has reached consensus, you may enlist the aid of someone with excellent writing skills to prepare a clear and compelling document that pulls it all together. That document is then vetted with the team and the larger audience before being finalized.

Your mission

Your mission defines your organization's purpose and focus beyond the basic financial motive common to for-profit businesses. Mission statements are often formatted as a verb phrase, e.g.:

Starship Enterprise's five year mission:

> *To explore strange new worlds; to seek out new life and new civilizations; to boldly go where no man has gone before.*

Ceres mission:

> *Integrating sustainability into day-to-day business practices for the health of the planet and its people.*

Google's mission:

> *To organize the world's information and make it universally accessible and useful.*

Your mission may be defined in terms of the scope of operation of your business—whom you serve, what needs you address, what means you use, and so forth. For instance, a fast-food chain may see its mission to provide affordable and satisfying meals for families of limited financial means. An educational program may seek to prepare future scientists to understand the potential environmental and health ramifications of their work through fieldwork and case studies.

Your mission may be unending, such as protecting a community, or it may be finite, ending when you have accomplished your objective, such as eradicating smallpox. A finite end may be more theoretical than practical, as in eliminating world hunger or poverty. Alternatively, the mission may be time-bound, such as the Starship Enterprise's mission cited above, and may be renewed subsequently or followed by a different but related mission, or the organization disbanded. For instance, an environmental coalition may seek to reduce greenhouse gas emissions worldwide by a certain percentage within a specific timeframe. If successful, it may set a new goal for further reductions, or it may turn to another pressing issue; if unsuccessful, it may adjust the target or narrow its focus to an underlying issue.

The most powerful mission statement is clear; distinctive—separating you from other similar organizations; and challenging—providing a source of inspiration to your employees and other stakeholders. Disney used to have a very succinct mission statement:

Make People Happy.

Although it lacked detail about how it would accomplish this mission, it certainly seems inspirational. Who wouldn't want to buy from, or go to work everyday for, an organization dedicated to making people happy? More recently their mission was changed to:[5]

To be one of the world's leading producers and providers of entertainment and information. Using our portfolio of brands to differentiate our content, services and consumer products, we seek to develop the most creative, innovative and profitable entertainment experiences and related products in the world.

Perhaps the newer statement is clearer and more distinctive, but it seems somewhat less inspiring. Ideally you want your mission statement to be both, e.g. (author's version):

We seek to make people happy by providing the most creative, innovative and profitable entertainment experiences and related products in the world.

---

[5] Source: http://www.missionstatements.com/fortune_500_mission_statements.html

Mission Statement Worksheet

What is your overarching objective?

What timeframe?

Whom do you serve?

Who is out of scope?

What needs do you address?

What is out of scope?

What means do you use?

What means are out of scope?

Key words or phrases essential to your mission:

Value-driven

Your values are the deeply held beliefs and timeless principles that define the character of your organization and guide its behavior. Your values are every bit as important as your mission in defining who you are as an organization. While we often label values with single words or phrases—integrity, service orientation, respect—we need to understand the deeper meaning underlying those words to ensure that everyone in the organization lives by them.

Deeply held beliefs are typically expressed as statements, such as "All men are created equal" or "Honesty is the best policy" or this book's underlying premise, "We're all in this together." Principles are generally expressed as rules to guide people's decisions and actions, such as "Honor your commitments" or "Look before you leap," or the Golden Rule: "Do unto others as you would have others do unto you."

You will recall that *value-driven* has two related meanings for your strategy—in addition to providing value by responding to the legitimate concerns of every stakeholder, it is based on certain core principles or values. While there are many important values that you may adopt as an organization, we will only highlight a few that are essential to a value-driven strategy:

- Integrity
- Mutual respect
- Service orientation
- Fairness
- Openness

Let us look at each of these values in turn.

Integrity

The most basic requirement for a value-driven strategy is integrity. Integrity means doing what is right, ethically and morally, even when it is difficult. It means honoring your commitments, taking responsibility for your actions, admitting your mistakes and acknowledging the contribution of others. As an organization with integrity, you take a leadership role in setting high standards, going beyond the minimum required by law or regulation. When a problem arises that affects your stakeholders, you step up and take initiative to fix it, regardless of who may have caused it. You do these things regardless of whether anyone else notices.

Mutual respect

A value-driven strategy is grounded in respect for your stakeholders—their human dignity, their ideas and concerns, their individual perspectives. You treat everyone equally with respect and courtesy, listen to their thoughts and concerns and strive to understand their point of view, and look for something positive in every idea. You test assumptions before you act, and you share the reasoning behind your decisions and actions. You foster an atmosphere of collaboration and teamwork, and thank each person for his or her contribution. You remain professional and unconditionally constructive with even the fiercest adversaries.

Service orientation

One of the values that set a value-driven strategy apart from others is a strong service orientation. It begins with the commitment to do no harm and then seeks to create as much value as possible for the greatest number. Organizations that embody this value are imbued with compassion and a spirit of generosity, acting as stewards of the environment and the community and seeking to ensure the well-being of others. Whenever your organization places others' interests and the common good ahead of your own, your social capital increases dramatically. This is especially so when you use whatever power you may have for the benefit of others rather than yourself.

Fairness

A sense of fair play is the cornerstone of a value-driven strategy. In striving to respond to the concerns of all your stakeholders, you inevitably encounter conflicting needs that must be reconciled. It is in such situations that evenhandedness comes into play. You first seek the "win-win" solution that leaves everyone better off. You take a systems view of the situation, looking at the big picture and considering the interdependencies, underlying causes and ramifications. You strive to strike an equitable balance among the parties through their active involvement in the process.

Openness

Being value-driven requires a degree of openness between your organization and your stakeholders. First and foremost, you must begin with a sincere desire to understand your stakeholders and their concerns, needs and perceptions. With a spirit of inquiry, you reach out constantly to engage your stakeholders, asking questions to further your insight, listening and observing carefully, and testing assumptions and confirming understanding. In return you offer them transparency, providing relevant information and sharing your thoughts, ideas, and concerns.

Your organizational values

Think about what these values mean to you. Call to mind other organizations you admire for their integrity, their respectful and fair treatment of others, their service orientation and openness. Reflect on your own experiences. When has someone acted in these ways toward you? Then recall examples when the opposite was true. Which role model would you rather emulate on behalf of your own stakeholders?

Consider the extent to which your organization's culture and actions embody these values. What other values are essential to your organization? Are your values an integral part of the fabric of the organization, or are they an afterthought? Are they merely given lip service, only to be forgotten or dismissed when matters become difficult? Think about how you embed these values in the organization. What policies and practices are essential to ensure that you are living your values? When you are clear about your mission and values, they become the bedrock of your strategy.

Your inviolable rules of engagement

It is one thing to espouse certain values, and quite another to actually live by them every day. Good intentions are not enough. It is your actions, not your words, that garner your social capital. What are the inviolable rules that govern the decisions and actions of everyone in your organization? Have they been clearly articulated and communicated? What are the consequences for anyone who fails to follow them? Do your leaders model the behaviors that the rules demand? If people within your organization are not prepared to live by the rules, either the people or the rules need to be changed. That is especially true of leaders.

The same is true of your mission. It describes not only the scope of your business, but also what falls outside of that scope. It can be tempting to accept every opportunity that comes your way, especially during difficult economic times, even when the work lies outside your area of focus. If you take on business or engage in activities that lie outside your mission, especially those for which you have no special capabilities, you risk diluting your brand and undermining your capital. Your stakeholders may no longer be certain what you stand for. To protect against this happening, it is helpful to establish ground rules for deciding what work you will accept and for tactfully redirecting all other work. If you feel you must take on unrelated work as a matter of survival or to explore a new avenue, you may wish either to revise your mission statement to encompass the change or to make it clear that this a temporary departure due to extraordinary circumstances.

Rules of Engagement Worksheet

Organizational Value	Inviolable Rule(s)	Consequences of Violating Rule(s)

Exercise 6: Envisioning the Future

The third strategic driver, after your mission and values, is your organization's vision for the future. Your vision creates a challenging and imaginative picture of what you hope to achieve, typically stated in the present tense, e.g.:

Steve Jobs:

> *"An Apple on every desk"*

JFK, Man on the Moon Speech, Joint Session of Congress May 25, 1961:

> *"I believe that this nation should commit itself to achieving the goal, before this decade is out, of landing a man on the moon and returning him safely to the earth."*

Your vision defines your strategic intent and aspirations. Aligned with your mission and values, it sets the direction for your organization for a specific time horizon, typically anywhere from three to ten years, but perhaps even twenty or more years in the future. Your vision should resonate with all members of the organization and inspire them to take action to make the vision a reality. Rather than a purely self-aggrandizing image, such as becoming the premier organization in your industry, the most compelling vision seeks to improve lives, to make a difference to your stakeholders—to customers, to communities, to the environment, to the world.

You may already have a vision statement, in which case you need only to review your progress and update or modify the vision as appropriate. However, if you do not have a vision currently, or if there has been a significant change in circumstances or focus, your organization may wish to create a new vision statement. As with the mission and values, the exercise should be a group effort, led by a core team and affirmed by the broader organization. The core team may be supported by an extended team comprising three to seven working groups, each focused on a separate stakeholder category or group.

Creating your vision

The visioning process itself is an exercise involving creative brainstorming. It requires letting go of the present in order to imagine a better future. There is often a strong emotional component to the exercise, as bold ideas are generated and hopes and fears are brought to the surface. As with the mission and values, it is more important to focus on the key elements than to worry about the precise wording. Once consensus has been reached about the crucial elements, the team can enlist a skilled writer to wordsmith a draft document for review.

While there are many ways to develop a vision for your organization, we will only describe one such method here. This particular method has been chosen because it focuses specifically on your stakeholders, hence is well-suited to a value-driven strategy.

Getting started

In preparation for the exercise, participants should review the groundwork that was laid during the previous exercises. In particular they will want to take note of the current gaps in your stakeholder relationships, possibilities for enhancing value to and from stakeholders, opportunities for creating a stakeholder community, and high priority changes to your business capital. This review may be done independently or together, or some combination. For participants who were involved in the previous exercises, this review will be brief; others will need time to absorb the information and reflect on its meaning.

Following the preparatory step, the core team selects a suitable timeframe for their visioning exercise. Most visions have a five to ten year time horizon, although there are some as short as three years and others as far out as twenty or thirty years. The long timeframes are designed to allow a break from the current status and to acknowledge that most changes take time to implement. On the other hand, a shorter duration creates a sense of urgency, requiring a high level of energy and intense effort over a briefer time period. Only you can decide what timeframe works for you.

Guiding principles

At this point the core team may also choose to establish a set of guiding principles to give shape to the visioning process. The guiding principles represent a synthesis of the possibilities for strengthening stakeholder relationships and maximizing the organization's business capital. For example, "Keep stakeholders informed of relevant matters in a timely manner." The specifics may vary for different stakeholders, but the guiding principles apply to all.

Defining the future for stakeholders

Next, participants project the business forward into the future by describing the viewpoints of your stakeholders. The core team may do this together, working sequentially, or they may assign different categories of stakeholders to separate working groups or business units. To help visualize each scenario, it may be easier to choose a representative member of each category—a key client, major supplier or specific environmental group, for example—and describe the scenario from their point of view.

While each stakeholder perspective will have its own set of concerns, the questions on the following page are typical of the types of topics your teams should address. Develop your own essential discussion points based on the in-depth analysis of your stakeholders during the Strategic Assessment phase.

(Complete one worksheet for each stakeholder group, plus one for the organization itself.)

Section 1 (same for all stakeholders):

Time Horizon:

Guiding Principles (same for all stakeholders):

Section 2 (unique for this stakeholder group):

Stakeholder/group:

Representative member (optional):

Synopsis of future state envisioned for this stakeholder/group:

Sample discussion points for envisioning the future:

Customers	Employees	Suppliers, Distributors, Strategic and Financial Stakeholders	Remaining stakeholders
Stakeholder experience			
• Who I am • What attracts me to your organization and keeps me coming back • What products and services I value and why • What touch points matter to me and why • How my needs and values align with your organization • What I expect you to know about me • What other organizations I consider buying from and why, and why I choose you	• Who I am • What attracts me to you as an employer, and why I remain with you • What strategic functions I serve and how that helps to differentiate your organization • What capabilities and/or competencies are required • How my role aligns with the organization's values and principles • What other employers I consider and why, and why I choose you	• Who I am • What attracts me to work with you, why I remain • What services I provide and how that helps to differentiate your business • What other organizations I serve and why, and why I work with you	• Who I am • What stake I have regarding your business • What I value about your organization • What value I provide to you and how that helps to differentiate your business • What other organizations I have a stake in and why, and why I prefer your organization
Key considerations			
• Who are your customers (new and existing)? Who are the decision makers? The influencers? What do you know about how they make purchase and other decisions? • How are you positioned in the marketplace? What is your value proposition? How will you attract customers? What will be your key selling points? • What are the organization's primary corporate strengths in the future? How do these differentiate the organization in the marketplace? • How do you achieve deep understanding of customer needs and values? How do you continuously refine and analyze this information? • What are your customer's experiences with the products you offer (the key features, the look-and-feel, the way you communicate with them)? • What are your customer's experiences with the way you interact (face-to-face, remote via personal channels, electronically)? How well integrated are the key touch points? • How do you manage relationships with your customers? Does this provide differentiation? • Who are your principal competitors in the future? How does their customer's experience differ from your customer's experience?	• Who are your employees (new and existing)? What motivates them? What do you know about how they make career decisions? • What are your recruiting and hiring practices? What is the degree of mobility for employees, both vertically and horizontally, within the organization? Do employees have a clear career path? What is your approach to personal development? How do these practices differentiate you in the employment marketplace? • What are your compensation policies? Other benefits? What sort of work environment do you provide? How do you compare with your competitors? • How do you reward and recognize good performance? How much responsibility do you give employees? How do you hold them accountable? What is your tolerance for risk taking? How do you respond when an employee makes a mistake? • What are the values that govern employee behaviors? What are the management practices that foster a positive working environment? How do you assess the climate of the organization? • What is your turnover rate? What compels employees to stay? When they leave, what are the primary reasons?	• Who are your key external stakeholders (new and existing)? What markets do they serve? Who are their other major relationships? How important is your relationship to them? • How do you select your suppliers, distributors or strategic stakeholders? What process do you use to evaluate potential suppliers, etc.? What criteria do you use? How often do you review the relationship? • How easy is it to work with you? How do you compare with other organizations? Why? • What financial arrangements do you have with them? Are payments settled promptly and fairly? Do they have a financial stake in the outcome of your business? • What do your suppliers, distributors, or strategic or financial stakeholders need from you? What are the touch points? What systems and processes do you share? • Do your suppliers, distributors, or strategic or financial stakeholders see you as integral to their success? Are they integral to yours? • Do your suppliers, distributors, or strategic or financial stakeholders feel that you treat them fairly? How do you address your differences? • How do you manage relationships with your stakeholders? Does this provide differentiation?	• Who are your key external stakeholders (new and existing)? What are their concerns? Who are their other major relationships? How important is your relationship to them? • What is the basis of your relationship with these stakeholders? How often do you review the relationship? • How easy is it to work with you? How do you compare with other organizations? Why? • What do your stakeholders need or want from you? What are the touch points? What systems and processes do you share? • What are your common challenges and objectives? • How do you manage relationships with your stakeholders? Does this provide differentiation? • Do your stakeholders see you as integral to their success? Are they integral to yours? • Do your suppliers, distributors or strategic stakeholders feel that you treat them fairly? How do you address your differences?
Essential points			

- What are the key sources of superior value you provide to the stakeholder? What are the key sources of value you receive from the stakeholder?
- What are the essential elements of the stakeholder experience that contribute a vital source of business capital, now and in the future?
- To what extent do these elements differentiate your organization from others?

Completing the picture

In addition to the stakeholder views, the team considers the internal and external sources and destroyers of business capital that were identified in the Expanded SWOT Analysis. Depending on the likelihood, urgency and importance of each situation, the team formulates an organizational view of the future in which those concerns have been addressed successfully.

Now is a good time to review your mission and values and identify any additional areas to be addressed. This step is especially useful when you first adopt the value-driven approach or when you have omitted certain stakeholders from your detailed visioning exercise. A quick review will help to identify and address any blind spots in your organizational vision.

Pulling it all together

Once these stakeholder and organizational viewpoints have been developed, the team and working groups review them together and makes changes as necessary to ensure that they are mutually compatible and suitably inspiring. Collectively they should resolve your major gaps and destroyers of capital, both current and future, while building your stakeholder community and leveraging the positive sources of capital.

To bring it all together, the team prepares a headline and narrative describing the successful achievement of your vision. The document describes the guiding principles, what you achieved and how it differentiates your organization's future relationships with your stakeholders. Before finalizing the vision, both the summary document and the detailed viewpoints are vetted with the broader organization.

Exercise 7: Strategy Mapping

The next exercise conducted by the core team translates your vision into clear objectives and identifies the strategies you will pursue to achieve them, along with the critical success factors that must be addressed.

Strategy mapping is a way of thinking through the details of your strategy and provides a visual tool for communicating the strategic plan, simply and effectively, to the rest of the organization. Developed by Robert Kaplan and David Norton of Harvard Business School, the approach is an outgrowth of their pioneering work on the balanced scorecard.[6] For those of you in the not-for-profit sector, it is similar to the theory of change approach, often used for developing solutions to complex social problems, in that it uncovers the underlying logic chain of preconditions and initiatives that lead to the desired outcomes.

Strategy mapping begins with your vision, translated into long-range objectives for your organization and your stakeholders. It then works backward to identify the best strategies, essential processes and critical success factors needed to bring about the desired changes. The strategy map makes explicit the cause-and-effect relationships between the fundamental building blocks of your strategy, as seen from four different perspectives[7]:

- Outcomes (also referred to as Strategic Outcomes)
- Stakeholders
- Processes
- Resources-and-Capabilities

A sample diagram of a generic strategy map is shown on the next page. Your vision, mission and values define the desired outcomes at the highest level; together with enhancements to your business capital, they form the Outcomes perspective.

NOTE: To conserve space on the visual map, you may wish to capture each idea with a few words or brief phrase, while providing a more detailed description in a separate narrative to accompany your vision document and strategy map. Similarly, you may choose to split the map into sections, with each section addressing a different category or group of stakeholders.

---

[6] Strategy Maps, Robert S. Kaplan and David P.Norton, Harvard Business School Press, 2004

[7] The first two perspectives have been modified from the original Financial and Customer perspectives to better reflect the equality among diverse stakeholders; the fourth perspective has been relabeled from Learning and Growth to encompass a greater breadth of capabilities.

Generic Strategy Map

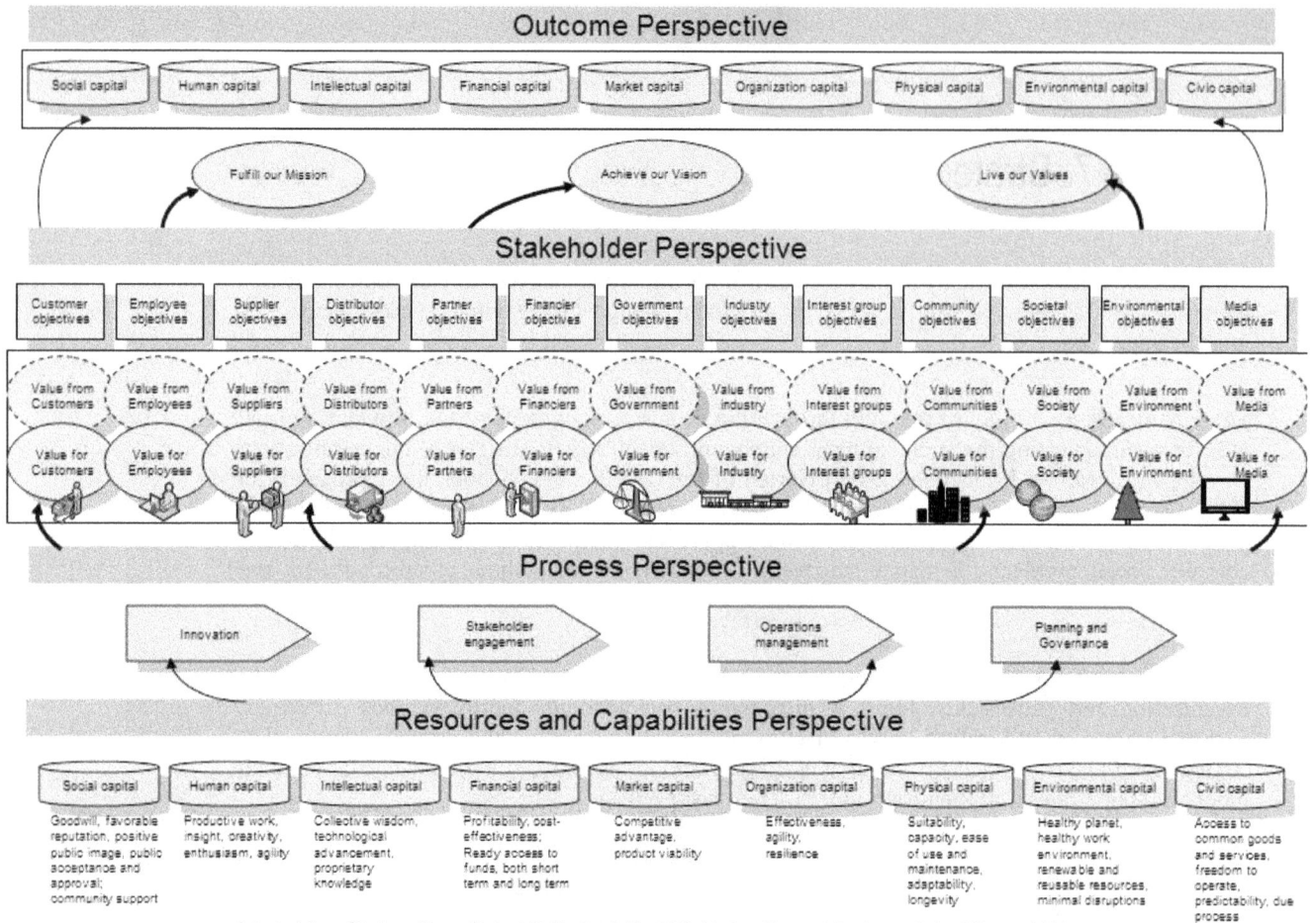

Outcome Perspective

| Social capital | Human capital | Intellectual capital | Financial capital | Market capital | Organization capital | Physical capital | Environmental capital | Civic capital |

Fulfill our Mission — Achieve our Vision — Live our Values

Stakeholder Perspective

| Customer objectives | Employee objectives | Supplier objectives | Distributor objectives | Partner objectives | Financier objectives | Government objectives | Industry objectives | Interest group objectives | Community objectives | Societal objectives | Environmental objectives | Media objectives |

Value from Customers / Value from Employees / Value from Suppliers / Value from Distributors / Value from Partners / Value from Financiers / Value from Government / Value from industry / Value from Interest groups / Value from Communities / Value from Society / Value from Environment / Value from Media

Value for Customers / Value for Employees / Value for Suppliers / Value for Distributors / Value for Partners / Value for Financiers / Value for Government / Value for Industry / Value for Interest groups / Value for Communities / Value for Society / Value for Environment / Value for Media

Process Perspective

Innovation — Stakeholder engagement — Operations management — Planning and Governance

Resources and Capabilities Perspective

Social capital	Human capital	Intellectual capital	Financial capital	Market capital	Organization capital	Physical capital	Environmental capital	Civic capital
Goodwill, favorable reputation, positive public image, public acceptance and approval; community support	Productive work, insight, creativity, enthusiasm, agility	Collective wisdom, technological advancement, proprietary knowledge	Profitability, cost-effectiveness; Ready access to funds, both short term and long term	Competitive advantage, product viability	Effectiveness, agility, resilience	Suitability, capacity, ease of use and maintenance, adaptability, longevity	Healthy planet, healthy work environment, renewable and reusable resources, minimal disruptions	Access to common goods and services, freedom to operate, predictability, due process

Adapted from *Strategy Maps*, Robert S. Kaplan & David P. Norton, Harvard Business School Press, 2004

Stakeholder and organizational objectives

The Stakeholder perspective translates your vision into specific stakeholder and organizational objectives. Your objectives are the qualitative results to be achieved in fulfilling your vision, often expressed as a verb phrase, e.g., "Provide custom solutions to our clients' needs at affordable prices" or "Create a work environment where employees can continue to learn and grow throughout their careers." The objectives encapsulate the stakeholder visions that you developed in the previous exercise.

The core team reviews your vision for your stakeholders and your organization and articulates a set of objectives that support your mission and values and infuse the vision. Some objectives will be specific to a certain stakeholder group, such as investors, while others may encompass multiple stakeholder groups, such as all public interest stakeholders—NGOs, educational institutions, media and so forth. Still others will address current and future situations, both internal and external, that affect your business capital, for example, accelerating technological developments within your field of interest.

Stakeholder value propositions and exchanges

Continuing with the Stakeholder perspective, the team identifies the key new ways in which you will provide value to your stakeholders and, as appropriate, where you will seek additional value from them. The choices you make are the pillars of your value-driven strategy.

The team reviews the possibilities you identified during the Strategic Assessment phase, as well as the crucial elements from your vision for key stakeholders and your organization. Which of these ideas are essential to your vision and have the greatest potential impact? Which are essential to protecting and building your business capital? The ideas you have chosen are added to the Stakeholder perspective of your map.

Strategic processes

To achieve the objectives you have chosen, the team identifies the crucial processes that together create value for your stakeholders and build your business capital. For example, organizations striving for innovative product leadership emphasize their research and development processes, while businesses committed to operational excellence emphasize such processes as workflow automation and resource management. Alternatively, if your organization is focused on achieving customer intimacy, you may place your greatest emphasis on customer relationship management, custom solutions and customer service.

To achieve your vision, at which processes must your organization excel? What new processes are required? The team considers various types of organization processes—innovation, stakeholder engagement, operations management, and planning and governance—and highlights the strategic process objectives in the next level of your strategy map, the Process perspective. To ensure completeness, the team reviews each stakeholder objective and value proposition and exchange to ensure that each is well supported by the processes you have identified.

Strategic resources and capabilities

Once you have defined the strategic processes essential to your vision, the team considers the business capital needed to achieve your objectives and identifies critical resource and capability gaps. What new or enhanced resources and capabilities are needed to support your strategic processes and achieve your vision? What new skills are needed to perform the new and enhanced processes? Does the organization have sufficient goodwill in the community to support the strategy? What new facilities, materials and equipment might be needed, and do you have sufficient financial resources? What additional funding do you need, and how will you obtain it? The team adds the critical success factors and resource and capability objectives to the final level of your strategy map, the Resources and Capabilities perspective.

Mapping the Future Worksheet

(Complete one worksheet for each stakeholder group, plus one for the organization itself.)

Stakeholder/group:

	Stakeholder objective(s)	Value to be provided	Value to be derived
Essential strategic processes			
Essential strategic resources and capabilities			

Closing the loop

Once again, the team conducts a final check of the logic chain, working backward, ensuring that each layer is adequately supported by the layer below it. The team then walks forward through the logic chain, and identifies the impact that successful achievement of the objectives, and ultimately the vision, will have on your business capital. The resulting enhancements to business capital are included as part of the Outcomes perspective.

If your strategy map is accompanied by a narrative, now is the time to pull it all together. The narrative helps describe the strategy in everyday language, emphasizing the crucial elements and linkages and articulating how the strategy achieves your vision. A well-written narrative includes the details necessarily omitted from the strategy map, and enables those who did not participate directly in the mapping process to understand the underlying logic.

Exercise 8: Strategic Scorecard

At this point you have defined your vision, established objectives, and devised strategies to achieve them. Your next step is to translate your strategic objectives into performance measures and establish your strategic scorecard, an approach pioneered by Robert Kaplan and David Norton of Harvard Business School. In this exercise, the team focuses on how best to measure the effectiveness of your strategy and monitor your progress toward achieving your vision. The team establishes targets for your desired outcomes and interim measures that provide feedback on your progress.

Outcomes and performance drivers

There are two types of performance measures—*leading* and *lagging*—that the team must consider. **Outcomes** are the tangible indicators of your ultimate success in achieving your strategic objectives; they measure results, hence, they are lagging indicators. **Performance drivers**, on the other hand, are leading indicators of the likelihood of success, tracked over the course of implementation, providing an early warning system that helps you stay on track. Outcome measures look backward, telling you what you have achieved, while performance drivers look forward, telling you whether you are on the right path. Both are essential to managing an effective strategy. (Outcomes in this context are not to be confused with the strategic Outcome perspective of your Strategy Map.)

At this point the team is not concerned with the numeric values to be achieved, only the type of metrics to use. How will you know when your objectives have been achieved? What tangible indicators would tell you whether you have been successful? For each objective, the team selects the most practical and meaningful outcome measure, typically expressed as a noun phrase, such as "the percentage increase in customer retention."

Because outcome measures are not sufficient to ensure success, the team also identifies performance drivers to monitor your progress. How will you know whether you are on track? What are the benchmarks that tell you whether you are making good progress toward your objectives? For each objective, the team identifies one or more practical measures that signal whether you are making sufficient progress. Like outcomes, performance drivers are typically expressed as a noun phrase, such as "number of days each month spent in the field by sales managers."

Goals and milestones

Once the outcomes and performance drivers have been identified, the team establishes specific target values for each, both short run and long run. They begin by establishing the ultimate goals to be achieved in your long-range planning horizon. Your goals are clear, concise and measurable results to be achieved by the end of the planning horizon, often expressed as a verb phrase or sentence, such as "Eliminate all known service gaps by year X" (outcome) or "Every sales manager spends a minimum of four days a month in the field" (performance driver).

In addition to the long term goals, the team establishes interim targets that mark progress toward the ultimate goal. These milestones are aggressive but realizable targets to be achieved by the end of a shorter planning period—typically a month, quarter or year—in order to be on track toward the longer-term goal, for example, "By the fourth quarter of Year 1, each sales manager is spending at least two days per month in the field."

Scorecard goals and milestones should be SMART—Specific, Measurable, Achievable, Realistic, Time-and-Resource Bound—and may include stretch goals. A simplified example of a generic strategy map and scorecard is shown below.

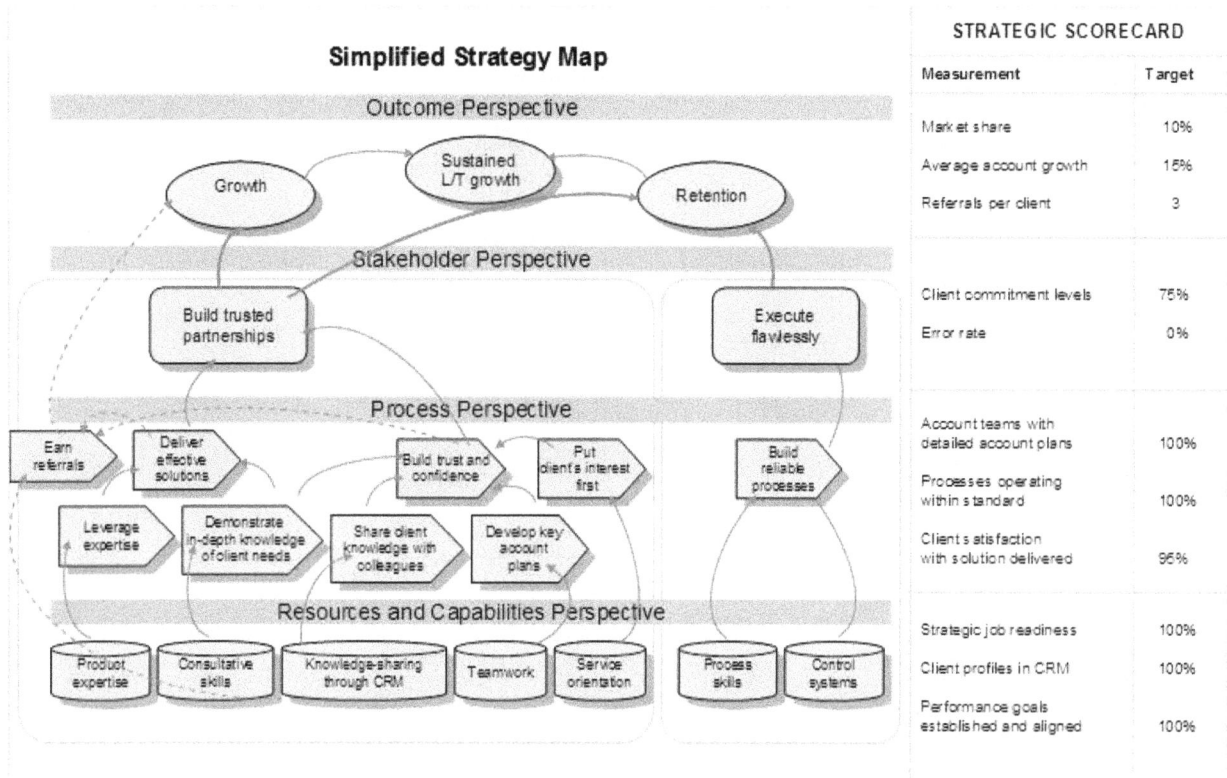

Simplified Strategy Map

STRATEGIC SCORECARD

Measurement	Target
Market share	10%
Average account growth	15%
Referrals per client	3
Client commitment levels	75%
Error rate	0%
Account teams with detailed account plans	100%
Processes operating within standard	100%
Client satisfaction with solution delivered	95%
Strategic job readiness	100%
Client profiles in CRM	100%
Performance goals established and aligned	100%

Strategic Scorecard Worksheet

Strategic Objective	Outcome measures (lagging indicators)				Performance drivers (leading indicators)			
	Metric	L/T Goal	Interim Milestone	Target date	Metric	L/T Goal	Interim Milestone	Target date

Part III: Strategy Implementation

In the previous step, you developed a cohesive picture of where you want to go as a business. The third step in planning is to choose your way forward and to ensure that the whole organization is on board and ready to move ahead. What new policies and initiatives are needed to execute the strategy? How much can we undertake at any given time? What should we do first? How will we get everyone on board? What preparations do we need to make?

In this section we introduce four new analytical exercises that can help your organization address these questions and ensure full integration of your strategy across your organization:

- **Exercise 9: Project Prioritization**
  A structured decision-making framework for selecting and prioritizing strategic initiatives and action plans in the face of resource constraints

- **Exercise 10: Strategic Alignment**
  A thorough analysis of the internal components of your organization and their effectiveness in supporting your strategy

- **Exercise 11: Organizational Change/Transformation**
  A method for preparing everyone within your organization to support the new strategic direction

- **Exercise 12: Cascading Goals**
  Translation of your organization's strategic goals into relevant performance goals for each group and individual

Exercise 9: Project Prioritization

In the previous exercises the team developed a full picture of the future and the pathway to reach it. In the next exercise, the team selects the policies and strategic initiatives that will bring your strategy to fruition. This process may be reasonably straightforward, with few conflicts or interdependencies among initiatives and with adequate resources in place, or it may be highly complex, with multiple interdependencies among projects and overwhelming demand on limited resources.

The greater the complexity and the more significant the changes required, the more important it is to have a structured process and decision-making framework. This is especially so when the strategy requires one or more large scale, multi-year projects that involve major system changes or significant training or staffing requirements.

While there are many ways to structure your process, we focus only on the basic principles here. It is up to your team to decide what level of analysis is relevant and useful to your organization.

Managing complexity

There are potentially three primary sources of complexity among your strategic initiatives:

- New lines of business or new, distinctly different markets, or other significant changes affecting specific areas of the organization

- Interdependencies among projects, e.g., deliverables from one project are needed as input to another

- Potential strain on shared resources, such as information technology, facilities, training and marketing, as well as funding

Each of these circumstances requires a phased approach to avoid undue stress on the organization and ensure a successful implementation. The three scenarios are depicted on the following pages.

For major changes that affect one or more parts of the organization, the team may propose a series of change initiatives, interspersed with periods of relative stability in which processes and systems are well-controlled and policies and structures are fully integrated. During each change initiative, processes and systems changes are aligned, tested and documented, new policies and structures are developed, and sufficient resources are developed to support the new processes. Monitoring is in place to ensure the changes become stabilized.

Basic Phased Implementation

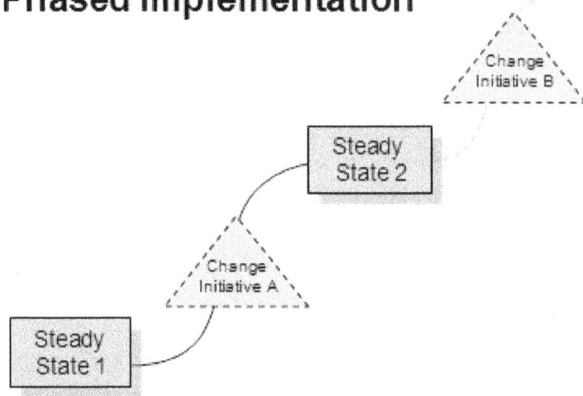

For initiatives that are interdependent, the team proposes a logical sequence that ensures that the necessary inputs are available for each initiative prior to its start. This approach may require projects to be done in strict sequence or may allow the projects to overlap, depending on the specific dependencies.

Project Interdependencies

Sequential:

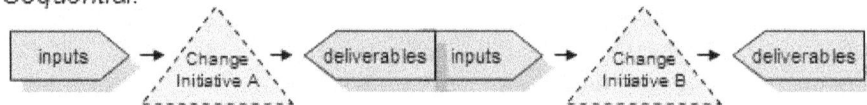

Overlapping:

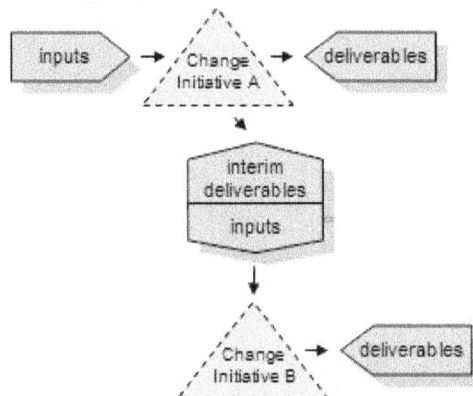

For projects that draw upon the same limited resources, even though they may be otherwise independent, the team may stagger the scheduling of initiatives so that the combined effort does not place undue strain on those resources.

Multiple Demands on Limited Resources

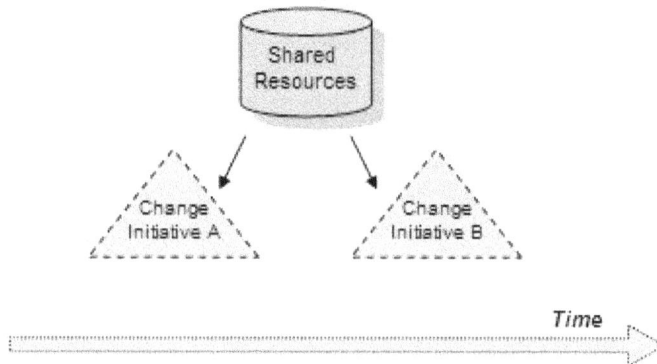

Project identification, selection and management

The core team reviews the strategy map to identify a series of initiatives that, taken together, put the strategy into action. Individual initiatives may be assigned to, or sponsored by, specific working groups or project teams, who develop proposed action plans and budgets and, if appropriate, prepare the business case. The core team then evaluates those plans and selects and prioritizes projects based on resource constraints and inter-dependencies. Depending on your organization's governance process, the team may be empowered to make the final decision or it may need to seek final approval from executive management or the board.

Project Proposal and Business Case

Project ideas typically originate from the core team or, in some cases, from other sponsors within your organization. Each initiative may address one or more aspects of your strategy, from closing the resource and capability gaps to designing and implementing your strategic processes and policies. Each project proposal provides a documented action plan, describing what actions are needed, who is involved and what resources are required. It sets forth a tentative timeline and any interdependencies with other initiatives, and makes the business case for supporting the initiative through funding and allocation of other resources.

In some cases, the project is straightforward, has no interdependencies and can be undertaken using existing resources; hence, a brief action plan, timeline and budget may suffice. Most of the time, however, projects—even the most desirable ones—must compete for resources and have interdependencies that force some projects to await the completion of others. In such situations, a more detailed proposal is necessary to enable the team to make decisions and establish priorities. Typical elements of a detailed proposal include the following:

- Project sponsor and team members
- Project overview (scope, objectives, projected impact, project duration)
- Strategic purpose
- Action plan
- Key deliverables, metrics and timelines

- Resource requirements
- Roles and responsibilities
- Risks
- Interdependencies
- Assumptions and constraints
- Cost/benefit analysis
- Alternatives and open issues, if any

Because the core team needs to be able to compare projects, it is important that everyone follow the same format and standards in preparing their proposals. Providing a template and brief guide can make the process easier to understand and follow.

For instance, your team may wish to provide guidelines for preparing certain elements such as metrics, resource requirements, risk assessment and cost/benefit analysis, including such parameters as labor costs and hurdle rates. Are current staff labor costs included or only incremental staffing? What about training? How are risks and non-financial costs and benefits to be assessed? How are revenues and cost savings estimated? How are capital investments amortized? How detailed must cash flow projections be, and over what timeframe? What are the measurable outcomes the initiative is likely to produce? A sample template is shown on the next page.

Project Proposal and Business Case - Executive Summary

General Project Information			
Business Sponsor		**Project Manager**	
Project Name			
Project Overview	*Briefly describe the project by summarizing the business need, the proposed solution and key deliverables. Attach detailed action plans as appropriate.*		

Strategic Impact

Briefly describe the impact on our stakeholder relationships and business capital.

Measurable Outcomes

Briefly state the impact on our strategic scorecard.

Estimated Resource Requirements

Area	Mktg/ Sales	R&D	Information Technology	Finance	Human Resources	Legal	Admin.	Senior Mgmt	External 1 (_____)	External 2 (_____)
Person-Months										

Financial Cost/Benefit Analysis Summary

	Year 1	Year 2	Year 3	Year 4	Year 5	Total
Capital investment						
Expenses:						
Labor						
Non-labor expenses						
Depreciation/amortization						
Total annual costs						
Financial benefits:						
Revenues						
Cost savings						
Total financial benefits						
Net cash flow						
					NPV at __%	

Interdependencies

Describe the interdependencies with other initiatives:
  - Decisions/deliverables/capabilities on which this initiative depends.
  - Elements of this initiative on which another depends.
  - Co-dependencies between initiatives, such as coordinated release dates, training, etc.

Strategic Alignment

Summarize the internal changes needed to bring the organization into alignment with the strategy. Note any potential conflict with other initiatives in this regard.

Risks

Summarize the key risks associated with this project, including the impact of any delays.

Assumptions and Constraints

Describe the crucial assumptions made in preparing this business case. How confident are we that these assumptions are correct? What is the impact if they are not?

Describe any constraints that may affect this project.

Proposal Review

When all projects have been submitted, the core team reviews the proposals and seeks clarification as needed. They then select and prioritize initiatives based on strategic fit, ease and impact, considering such issues as compatibility and interdependencies between projects, overlapping resource demands relative to capacity, the acceptable level of risks, and the reasonable distribution of effort across the organization. Projects to launch the rollout of the strategy are necessarily given top priority.

Methods vary for selecting projects under resource constraints and depend on your organizational culture and customary decision-making process. The core team may be comfortable reaching consensus through informal roundtable discussion, or you may prefer to establish formal criteria for evaluating projects, with assigned weights, against which each project is scored, as in the sample model below. If you choose to use such an approach, the team is encouraged to review the resulting project rankings against their intuitive sense, discuss any disconnects and adjust the rankings (and perhaps the criteria or weights as well) accordingly. Because no tool can anticipate every subtle issue that may arise, the team should not let the limitations of the tool constrain your decisions.

Sample Project Scoring Model

Project Name:
Business Sponsor: _____   Project Manager: _____

Necessity		Stakeholder Impact		Business Capital Impact		Ease to Implement		Affordability		Risk	
Investment is necessary to comply with regulatory, legal or ethical requirements, or to honor our corporate mission and values.		Investment supports strategic direction of the company.		Investment protects and enhances essential business capital, improving our sustainability		Investment is within our organizational capacity		Investment is financially sound and cost-effective, and fits within our financial capacity		Investment is within tolerable levels of risk	
Not required	0	Investment does not support a strategic objective	0	Investment does not affect our business capital	0	Investment is apt to overwhelm our organizational capacity or is totally dependent on other initiatives	0	Investment is significant for the benefits obtained	0	Investment has significant upside potential; minimal downside risk	0
Not required but desirable business practice	1	Investment supports strategic objectives of one stakeholder or group	1	Investment improves somewhat our ability to compete	1	Investment significantly stresses our capacity or is dependent on other initiatives	1	Investment is financially sound but costs are substantial and payback is lengthy	1	Investment has minimal or moderate upside potential; minimal downside risk	1
Under serious consideration for future passage into law or regulation, not likely within the next fiscal year	2	Investment supports strategic objectives of more than stakeholder or group	2	Investment improves moderately our business capital	2	Investment significantly stresses our capacity in the short run but is independent of other initiatives	2	Investment is financially sound with shorter payback, but costs are substantial	2	Investment has significant upside potential; moderate downside risk	2
Likely to be required by law or regulation within the next fiscal year	3	Investment supports strategic objectives of most or all stakeholders	3	Investment improves significantly our business capital	3	Investment moderately stresses our capacity in the short run and is independent of other initiatives	3	Investment is financially sound and costs are moderate	3	Investment has minimal or moderate upside potential; moderate downside risk	3
Required by law or regulation, but not during the next fiscal year	4	Investment is a pre-requisite for other essential strategic initiatives	4	Investment provides clear competitive advantage	4	Investment moderately stresses our capacity but is important to other initiatives	4	Investment is low cost or ultimately self-funding	4	Investment has significant upside potential as well as significant downside risk	4
Mandated by law or regulation or essential to our corporate mission and values	5	Investment is essential to execution of corporate strategy and to ensuring our sustainability	5	Investment provides world-class capability	5	Investment is well within our organizational capacity or is essential to another initiative	5	Investment helps fund other initiatives	5	Investment has minimal upside potential; significant downside risk	5
wgt. X 0.4 = 0		wgt. X 0.1 = 0		wgt. X 0.1 = 0		wgt. X 0.1 = 0		wgt. X 0.3 = 0		wgt. X -0.4 = 0	

0

Project Coordination and Monitoring

Once projects have been approved, the core team establishes a master schedule for all projects, based on interdependencies and resource constraints and bottlenecks. Depending on your organization's structure, the core team may assume the project oversight role, or assign the responsibility to an administrative or project management office. Whichever group assumes the role monitors the progress of the strategic initiatives, resolves scheduling conflicts and resource constraints that arise, reviews and approves any change requests, and reports back at regular intervals to the core team and senior management.

Dynamic Process

The longer your planning time horizon, the more likely you will encounter unexpected events or significant shifts in circumstances that change your objectives or alter your priorities. The core team meets regularly to review the strategy and make whatever adjustments are necessary.

That said, major adjustments should be kept to a minimum to avoid disruption of the organization's momentum. Frequent, large-scale, unplanned changes can be demoralizing to the organization, weakening employee commitment and eroding your human capital. Ideally, the team considered the possibility of such developments during the expanded SWOT analysis and made allowances for contingencies in formulating the strategy. If so, making adjustments down the line will not be overly disruptive to the overall momentum, as they will be recognized as mere tweaks to the overall strategy.

However, if a new development occurs that was not anticipated, it could have significant impact on the organization's momentum. For this reason it is vital that the team has done its homework thoroughly to minimize the likelihood of surprise, and that every effort is made to keep the organization on track should an unanticipated development occur. A key part of this effort is maintaining open communications with employees and other affected stakeholders. We will take a closer look at the communications process in Exercise 11: Organizational Change/Transformation.

Exercise 10: Strategic Alignment

It is often said that "the devil is in the details," and this is especially so for successful implementation of your strategy. Thus far we have taken a macro view of your strategy, establishing the overall direction and approach and creating a series of initiatives to get you where you want to go. However, unless every internal aspect of your business is aligned and integrated with your strategy, you are unlikely to achieve complete success. At best, you may waste time and resources in counter-productive activity, delaying or preventing you from reaching your goals. At worst, you may fail to make any progress at all, as the organization seizes up in the midst of confusion and cross-purposes. This next exercise is intended to help ensure your organizational effectiveness by aligning all aspects of your internal organization to support your strategy.

Internal components

There are many different ways to characterize the internal workings of your organization. The model described below has proved helpful to other organizations; however, you are encouraged to choose whatever internal representation works best for your own organization. For discussion purposes, we break down components into the following general categories:

- Processes and management practices
- Systems, structures and policies
- Roles and responsibilities
- Abilities, behaviors and culture
- Tools, information and resources

Processes and management practices include all of the governance, innovation, relationship and operational processes of your business, as well as the management and leadership practices employed at every level of your organization. Examples of the latter include such practices as "managing by walking around", "walking the talk", consensus-building and collaboration, and open communications, to name a few.

Systems, structures and policies include such formalized matters as the reporting hierarchy, including the span of control, number of levels and breakdown along functional, business and geographic lines; designation of decision-making authority; coordinating mechanisms; compliance and controls; and various human resource policies and systems, such as paid time off and performance management.

Roles and responsibilities include such formal elements as job design and career paths, as well as more fluid, temporary roles, such as participation on committees, task forces and project teams.

Abilities, behaviors and culture include such elements as individual skills, knowledge, and attitudes; interpersonal relationships and informal work arrangements; organizational climate, behavioral norms and language; and the organization's history and self-image.

Tools, information and resources include the physical work environment; various management information systems and knowledge sharing tools; financial, physical and other resources.

Internal congruence

To maximize the likelihood that your strategy will be successful, all of your internal components need to be in close alignment with one another and with your strategic drivers. Typically people within the organization may find themselves working at cross-purposes, bumping into one another in a kind of Brownian motion. Imagine instead the power of having everyone in your organization moving in the same direction. Your strategic drivers—mission and values, vision, goals and objectives—provide a beacon for everyone to follow.

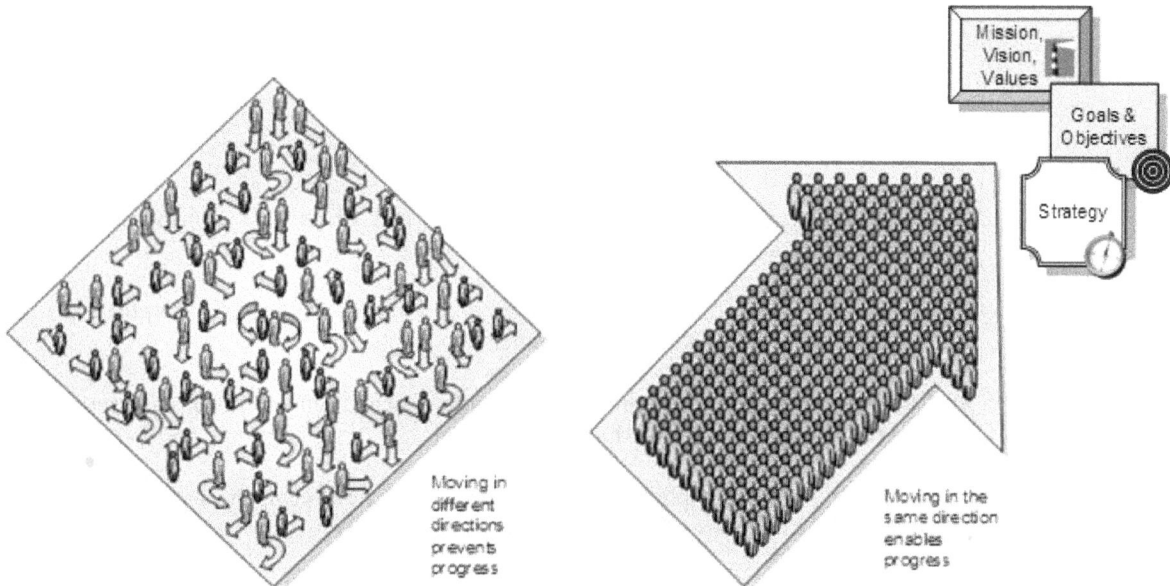

Moving in different directions prevents progress

Moving in the same direction enables progress

The same holds true for the non-human components, such as the building layout and information systems; when they are aligned with the strategic drivers, they guide behavior toward the desired outcomes. When components are mutually compatible or synergistic, they maximize your organization's effectiveness.

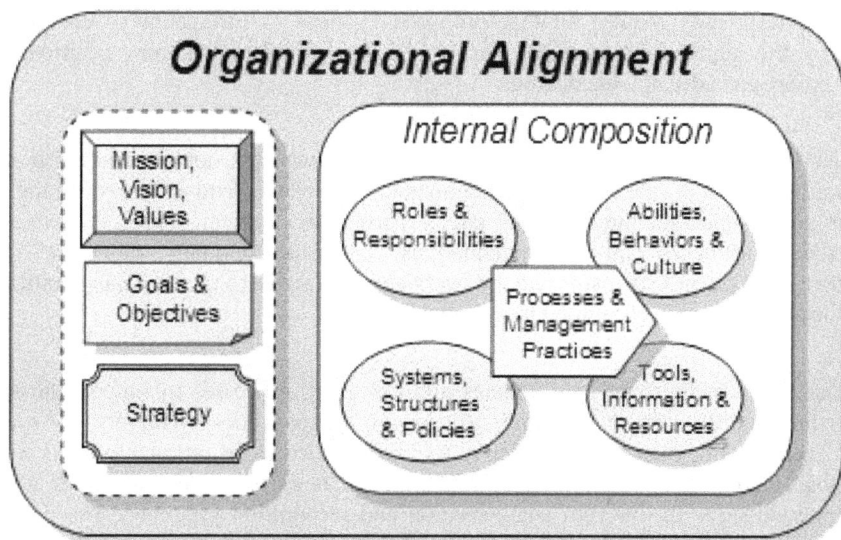

Organizational Alignment

Internal Composition

Mission, Vision, Values

Goals & Objectives

Strategy

Roles & Responsibilities

Abilities, Behaviors & Culture

Processes & Management Practices

Systems, Structures & Policies

Tools, Information & Resources

Generally the degree of alignment between any two components, or between a component and a strategic driver, will fall into one of the following categories:

- **Conflict** – the components and/or driver are mutually incompatible; the component undermines the strategy or the components work at cross-purposes (other than situations where one is intended to modulate the effect of the other).

  Example: Employees are assigned to work as a team but are rated individually on a curve when the time comes to hand out bonuses.

- **Neutrality** – the components, or component and driver, are compatible, but the component(s) neither impede nor advance the strategy.

  Example: Tuition reimbursement continues to support individual development needs and interests, irrespective of the business strategy.

- **Harmony** – the components, or component and driver, are compatible and each component is designed to advance the strategy.

  Example: Procedures are revised and group training is conducted to implement a new policy for expedited handling of customer complaints.

- **Synergy** – the components are mutually reinforcing and actively advance the strategy and accelerate progress toward achieving the vision.

  Example: A new public relations position and new company-wide processes are established to increase transparency and respond sensitively to online bloggers and media critics.

Alignment process

Strategic alignment may be addressed on two levels—within each individual initiative and across the entire organization—throughout the implementation. Depending on the scope of anticipated changes, the core team may establish a separate task force to oversee the alignment process. The oversight team conducts an initial review and establishes guidelines to the project teams. For instance, the team may require all that proposed changes to headcount or compensation be reviewed by the human resources department, or may stipulate that new positions be filled internally before considering outside hires.

Each project team includes a review of alignment in its own work domain and either makes the necessary adjustments or makes recommendations to be reviewed and approved by the oversight team. (For an example, see the following page.) Throughout implementation the oversight team reviews the adjustments and recommendations to ensure ongoing alignment across the organization. Both the project teams and the oversight team strive to eliminate any conflicts and to increase the synergistic effects among the components.

For instance, after establishing new policies and designing processes to support the strategy, a team may find that the current reporting structure no longer works effectively. The work may require the creation of new positions which in turn require new skills or knowledge as well as new career paths. Current staff members who assume these new roles may need skills training and suitable tools, along with different compensation and recognition programs. The new structure may require different coordinating mechanisms and management practices, aided by new reports or information systems.

All of these changes may conflict with the existing culture of the organization—for example, moving from a culture of star performers to a collaborative environment—one of the more challenging situations you are likely to face. The next exercise helps address such significant organizational changes.

Sample review of internal congruence:

Strategic Initiative: *Transform sales organization from strictly geographic to industry focus for major accounts*								
	Internal Element	Degree of alignment (<u>S</u>tatus/<u>T</u>arget)				Changes needed	Effort	Impact
		Conflict	Neutral	Harmony	Synergy			
Roles and responsibilities	Sales job description	S	☐	☐	->T	Revamp to distinguish industry specialists from small account managers	M	H
	Customer service support role	S	☐	☐	->T	Revamp to match sales	H	H
	Sales manager role	☐	S	->T	☐	Realign assignments of direct reports	L	M
Abilities, behaviors and culture	Sales/service – industry specialists	☐	☐	☐	T	Select and train specialists	H	H
	Sales/service – small accounts	☐	☐	T	☐	Create job enrichment for junior staff members	H	M
Processes and management practices	Performance management	S	☐	☐	->T	Revamp to match new roles	H	H
	Sales reports	S	☐	☐	->T	Revamp to match new roles	H	H
	Marketing campaigns	☐	S	☐	->T	Develop industry specific campaigns	M	H
Systems, structures and policies	Field service calls	☐	☐	T	☐	Develop protocol for partnering between industry account team and local account team	M	M
	Travel policies	☐	☐	T	☐	Create new travel allowances for industry account managers	M	M
Tools, information and resources	CRM system	☐	S	☐	->T	Add filter for industry view	L	M
	Sales tracking system	S	☐	☐	->T	Revamp to match new structure	H	H

Exercise 11: Organizational Change/Transformation

To be truly effective, your strategic drivers must become assimilated into the organization's culture. The greater the change from your current culture, the more crucial the need to engage everyone in the transformation and to take steps to ensure the changes are fully embedded in the attitudes and behaviors of your employees and managers.

Typically the transformation takes place over time. In the early stage the emphasis is on creating clarity and alignment of purpose across your organization, engaging managers and employees and getting them on board. In the middle stage, the emphasis shifts to mobilizing resources and integrating the changes into the fabric of your organization. Alignment continues throughout this stage, although at a more moderate level of effort. Meanwhile the momentum toward your goals continues to build.

In the later stage, the transformation accelerates. Old patterns of behavior have been replaced by new, resistance to change has diminished, and your organization is moving full steam ahead. Throughout the transformation, the monitoring process ensures that your organization continues to adapt dynamically to changing circumstances.

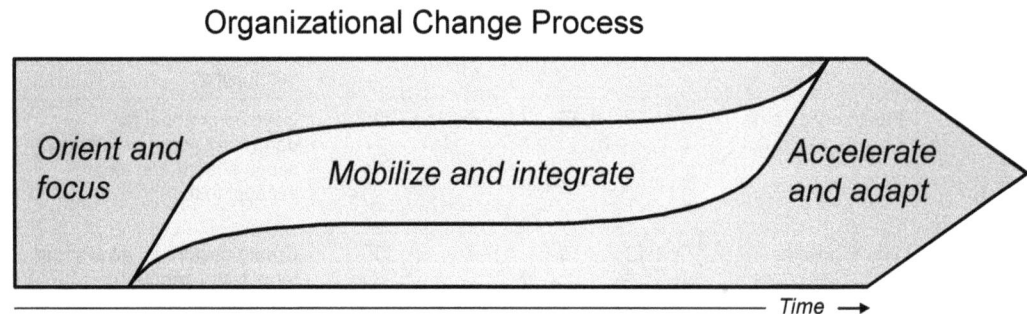

Organizational Change Process

Considerable planning has already begun to ensure your organization's alignment and to mobilize the organization toward implementation. Translating that planning into action is best served by conducting an effective organization-wide launch, followed by a sustained effort to keep people engaged and to gather valuable feedback from them. The process described below has been used successfully by both large and small organizations; you are encouraged to adapt it to the needs of your own organization.

Multi-pronged approach

The purpose of the exercise is to create a common understanding of your mission, values and rules of engagement, as well as your vision for the future and your reasons for adopting a value-driven strategy. It introduces the value-driven framework that underlies your strategy and provides a common language to refine and reinforce the concepts throughout your organization. In addition, it provides opportunities for managers and employees to respond to and assimilate the changes needed to implement your strategy.

There are three primary components to the approach:

- Leadership workshop(s) for managers at all levels
- Strategic orientation session(s) for all employees
- Manager-led employee work sessions for individual work units

The three components are mutually reinforcing and help to ensure a consistent message across the organization. When they occur within a coordinated timeframe, they also help build the momentum toward a sustainable transformation.

Leadership Workshop

Leaders throughout your organization are responsible for communicating the strategic direction on a regular basis, clearly and consistently, creating narratives that illustrate the intent in a meaningful way, acting as role models by embodying the principles in their own actions, and aligning individual objectives—their own as well as their employees'—with the organization's vision. The change initiative will succeed or fail based on the commitment and actions of your leaders. It is up to each of them to become personally committed to making change happen.

To help them do this and ensure consistency across the organization, leaders across the organization are brought together for one or more workshops. The workshops are most effective when they are completed across all locations within a short timeframe, previewing the official company-wide launch of the change initiative.

The objectives of the leadership workshops are threefold:

- Focus all leaders throughout your organization on the new direction the organization is taking and its importance
- Teach specific management practices and behaviors that create a supportive environment for the effort
- Prepare managers to lead a series of workshops with employees in their respective units

Strategic Orientation

The strategic orientation lays the foundation for the remaining rollout and ensures that everyone is on the same page. If possible, the orientation should be conducted live across the entire organization or by geographic location; alternatively, the key message may be presented via recorded video, followed by an interactive question-and-answer session with senior managers. In addition, written and on-line materials may be provided to each employee, summarizing the key points.

The content is the same no matter what delivery format you choose, depending upon your organization's particular circumstances, and the message is delivered by the chief executive and reinforced by other members of the senior management team. The orientation addresses the following:

- Your mission, values and rules of engagement

- The value-driven framework and its relevance to your organization's strategy

- Your vision of the future and the importance of having everyone pulling in the same direction

- What to expect as the implementation proceeds, including the employee work sessions, cascading of goals (next exercise), and the strategic initiatives and governance process, as well as any planned communication with external stakeholders regarding the strategy

An important aspect of the orientation is the opportunity for employees to ask questions and provide feedback. Their concerns and ideas, along with the appropriate responses, are then summarized and shared across the organization through the internal website or other communication channels. This process remains ongoing during the rollout and may continue throughout the implementation.

Employee Work Sessions

Managers throughout your organization lead a series of work sessions with their respective units, helping to embed the values, concepts and behaviors within the fabric of the organization. The sessions, which typically last no longer than thirty or forty minutes each, are held on-site at the unit's work location. The managers' role is to lead discussions and simple exercises that relate the concepts to the work their employees perform regularly within the organization.

The purpose of the work sessions is for employees to:

- Understand the business strategy and appreciate the rationale

- Identify areas of contribution for themselves and their unit

- See personal value in the changes being sought and make a commitment to act

Content may be provided via recorded video or other materials to ensure consistency and to relieve managers of the need to present the content themselves. In addition, managers have a leader's guide for each session, along with exercise materials as appropriate, provided during the leadership workshop held earlier.

The number of work sessions and specific content depends upon your strategy and the unique needs of your organization. For instance, each session may focus on a specific element of your strategy, one of the values and its corresponding rules of engagement, or a new skill or bit of knowledge that enables employees to better perform their roles. At least one of the sessions may focus on the strategic scorecard and how individual and unit goals can support the organization's goals (see the following exercise). Each session follows a similar format:

- Overview of relevant concepts

- Participative discussion

- Practice exercise in applying the concepts to the unit's work

- Optional assignment for further application

As you move into the mobilization stage, you may find it beneficial to continue these work sessions across the organization as a means of maintaining alignment, building momentum and ensuring a dynamic process. For instance, topics for future work sessions may be generated through feedback from stakeholders and focused on addressing their most crucial concerns.

Exercise 12: Cascading Goals and Objectives

During strategy formulation, your core team established a set of objectives, goals and milestones to achieve throughout the planning time horizon. Typically achieving these goals depends upon the collective efforts of people throughout your organization. Alignment of individual and group goals and objectives to those of your business as a whole is an essential part of your strategic implementation.

Beginning with the strategic scorecard, each area or strategic initiative identifies those goals and objectives to which it can and must contribute, and sets a corresponding set of goals and objectives for its own performance. The core team works with the area managers and project sponsors to ensure that, collectively, if everyone achieves their respective targets, the overall goal will be met or exceeded. This process is most effective when it is done collaboratively, both within the individual areas or project teams, as well as among the area managers and project sponsors.

As each level establishes its own scorecard in support of the strategy, the process is repeated at the next level down, continuing the cascading process until every person has goals that link to the organization's strategic goals. At each iteration, the senior manager works with his or her direct reports to ensure that the group's goals are fully supported and that none are in conflict with the overall strategic goals of your organization.

Linkages Throughout the Organization

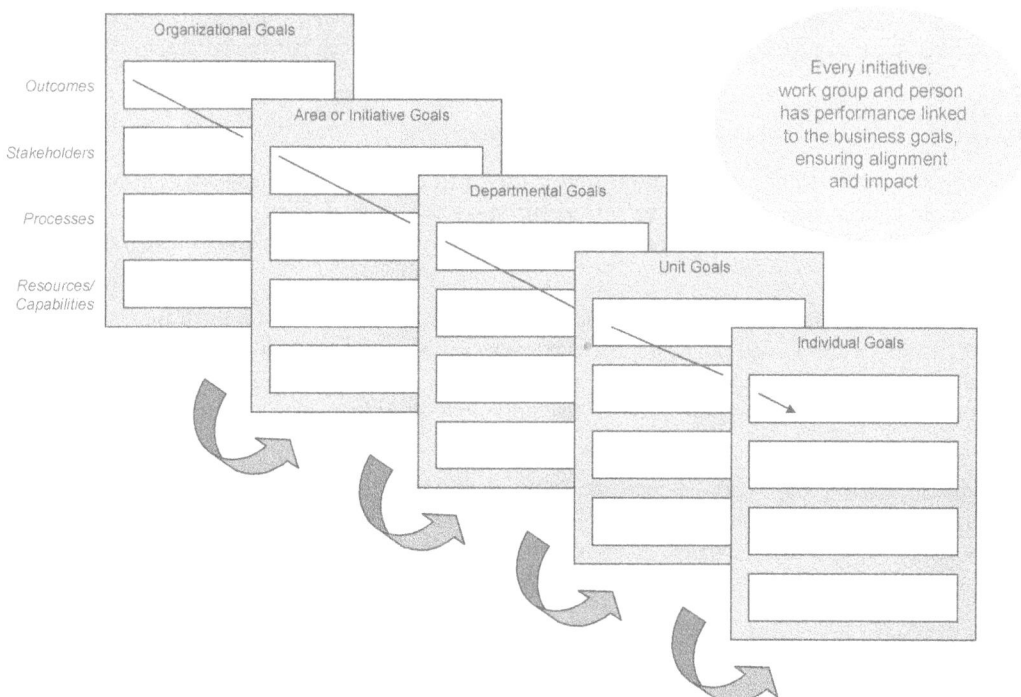

Outcomes

Stakeholders

Processes

Resources/
Capabilities

Organizational Goals

Area or Initiative Goals

Departmental Goals

Unit Goals

Individual Goals

Every initiative, work group and person has performance linked to the business goals, ensuring alignment and impact

In the interest of deepening employee understanding of the linkages between their work and your strategy, you are encouraged to select one or more examples of individual goals to share across the organization, as illustrated below. The examples chosen should be understandable for people in other functional areas and should illustrate clearly the linkages through each level of the organization. Ideally the individuals involved are the ones who make the presentation; in any case, the individuals must be comfortable having their goals shared with their associates.

Sample Cascading Goals

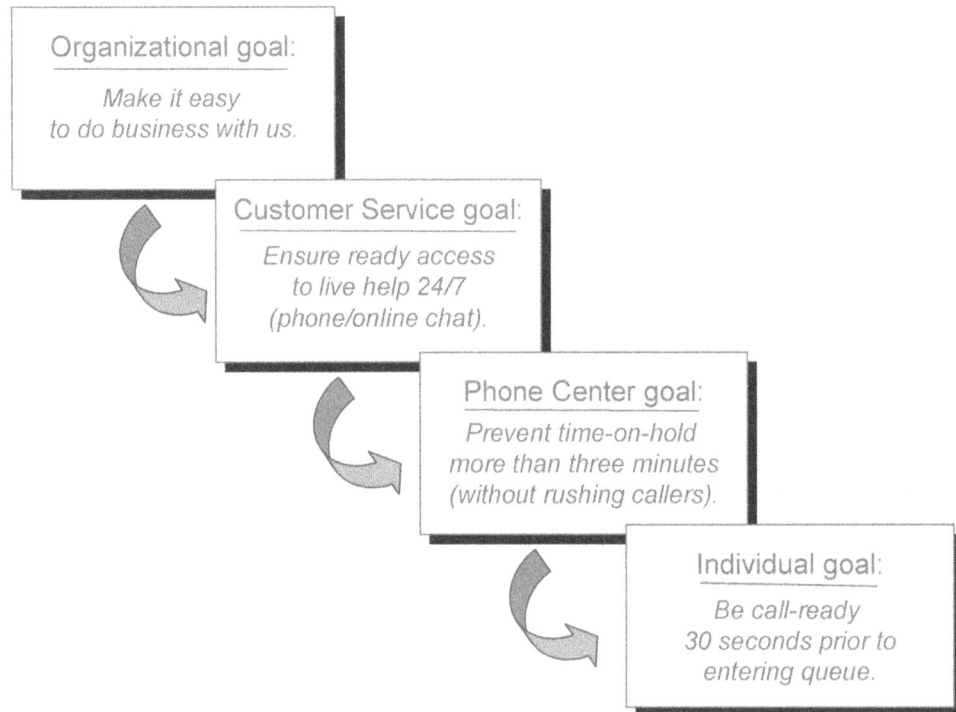

Organizational goal:

Make it easy to do business with us.

Customer Service goal:

Ensure ready access to live help 24/7 (phone/online chat).

Phone Center goal:

Prevent time-on-hold more than three minutes (without rushing callers).

Individual goal:

Be call-ready 30 seconds prior to entering queue.

Group level process

In addition to goal-setting, groups often find it useful to establish their own mission and vision statement to reflect their own role in your organization's strategy. Doing so makes the corporate mission and vision more meaningful to employees and provides a greater sense of ownership.

As specific performance goals are established, the group may discover that new skills, knowledge, tools or resources are needed to accomplish the goals that were not explicitly identified by the core team during the previous exercises. These needs must be addressed as well and may give rise to additional goals for the group as a whole or for individual development.

In addition, each group may choose to establish specific action plans for achieving their objectives. If these action plans require organizational resources not readily available, the group may be required to submit their plan and business case to the strategic oversight team for approval.

Case Study

WasteNot WantNot is a fictitious waste management company, providing trash pickup and recycling services to local communities and reselling recovered materials to manufacturers. The company operates multiple transfer stations and landfills throughout the areas they serve. They are seeking to expand their markets and to increase their positive impact on the environment, and are considering a number of new initiatives, such as composting and landfill transformation, among others. The following summary highlights the results of their strategic planning process.

Stakeholder Analysis

WasteNot WantNot began their process by taking a close look at their stakeholders, current and potential, and identifying their needs and concerns and ways to better serve them. The diagram below provides a snapshot of their key stakeholders (current and potential), while the table on the next page outlines their concerns and possible improvements, along with an estimate of their ease and potential impact.

WasteNot WantNot's Stakeholders

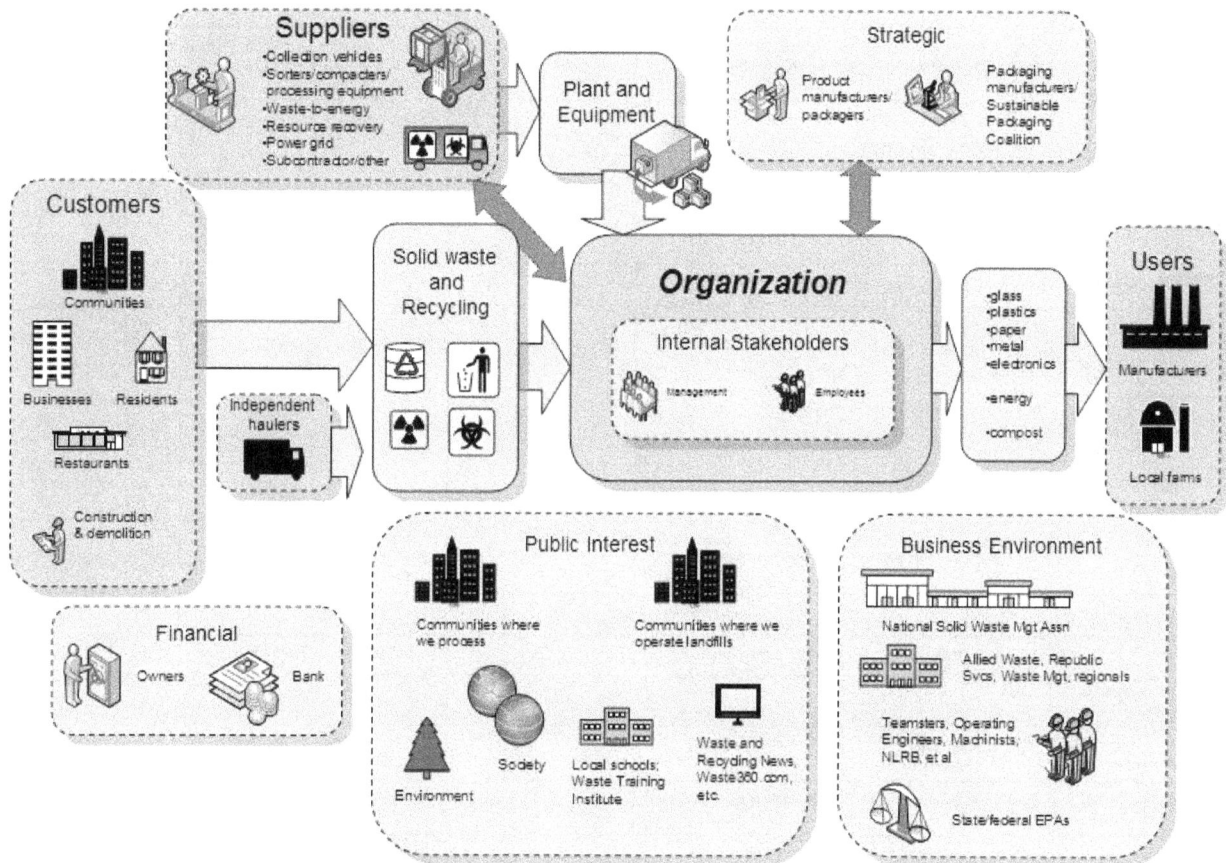

WasteNot WantNot Examples of Stakeholder Value

Stakeholder/Role	What they want	What they can provide	Gaps/ barriers/ issues (if any)	Strategic Possibilities	Effort	Impact
Customers (Waste Generators)						
Local communities	More compliance by residents and businesses; lower costs	Increased recycling, less un-recycled solid waste	Regions 1 & 3 separation required, fewer plastic types accepted	Single stream recycling; cost for trash versus pay for recycling; composting	M	H
Residents	Convenience, easy to use	Increased recycling		Single stream recycling	M	H
Business clients	Convenience; better containers; frequent pickup	Increased recycling	High percentage of cartons	Single stream recycling; containers/dumpsters; flex schedule; composting	M	H
Restaurants	Convenience; prevent vermin/ other sanitation issues	Separation of compostables	High organic content	Composting; specialized containers; redistribute usable food to shelters/needy	L	H
Construction and demolition clients	Convenience; lower cost	Increased recycling; separate hazardous waste	Limited time on job site makes recycling low priority	Single stream recycling; flex schedule	M/H	H
Independent haulers	Quick turnaround; flexible schedule; partial and combined loads	Full loads; prompt arrivals; preparedness; complete and accurate documentation	Documentation requirements; sorting for certain regions	Accept single stream recycling; offer incentive for full loads; support mobile technology for recordkeeping	M	M
Customers (Purchasers of Recycled Materials)						
Glass container manufacturers	Pre-sorted bundles	Understanding of how materials are used		Improve material recovery through finer sorting and chemical processing	M/H	H
Paper mills						
Plastic users						
Scrap metal users						
Electronic manufacturers						
Local farms	Good compost selection from diverse identified sources	Market for compost; food for local restaurants		Partner with local restaurants to provide each other compost or produce	L	H
Suppliers						
Suppliers – processing equipment (sorting, baling, etc.)	More business; maintenance contracts	Single stream processing; advanced sorting		Install new single stream processing equipment	M	H
Suppliers – resource recovery equipment	Shared knowledge	Improved technology		Partner with them to develop material recovery technology	H	H
Suppliers – waste to energy equipment	New business	Technology and expertise		Partner with them to generate energy from waste	H	H
Energy grid	Manage peak demand	Reduced utility rates		Generate energy from waste; sell excess to grid	H	H
Suppliers – collection vehicles	Repeat business; referrals	Conversion to hybrid or electric		Upgrade fleet, give them first dibs	L	H
Suppliers – hazardous waste subcontractor	Proper handling; business referrals	Proper handling; 24 hour emergency response		Provide referrals as appropriate	L	L
Other suppliers	Steady business; reduced paperwork	Competitive pricing		Maintain preferred supplier program; use electronic interface to minimize paperwork	L	M

WasteNot WantNot Examples of Stakeholder Value (continued)

Stakeholder/Role	What they want	What they can provide	Gaps/ barriers/ issues	Strategic Possibilities	Effort	Impact
Packaging Industry						
Product manufacturers/ packagers	Lower costs; product safety; convenience	Less packaging; sustainable packaging use		Partner with members of industry to reduce packaging waste	H	H
Packaging manufacturers	Protect revenues; lower costs	Sustainable packaging with labeling				
Sustainable Packaging Coalition	Closed loop cycles, sustainable design	Expertise				
Special Interests (Environment)						
licenses	Compliance with regulations	licenses		Engage stakeholders regularly	L	M
Environmental groups/ Wildlife habitats	Reduce waste, emissions, energy consumption	Feedback			L	M
Local schools; Waste Training Institute	Education	Mutual support		Educate the public regarding waste management	L	M
Communities and businesses where we process	Minimal noise and traffic disruptions; protection of health and safety; jobs and tax revenues; enhanced quality of life	Licenses and permits		Engage stakeholders in our initiatives and activities to gain insights and earn their support	L	M
Communities where we operate landfills				Transform closed landfills to public use	H	H
Other Stakeholders						
Employees/Unions (Teamsters, AFSCME, Longshoremen, Operating Engineers, Machinists, NLRB)	Job security, health benefits	Mutual understanding; good faith bargaining		Maintain good relationships through ongoing two-way communications; provide job security	L	M
Non-union employees/ managers	Professional growth	Innovation and teamwork		Provide growth opportunities through participation on strategic initiatives	L	M
Owners/bankers	Good return on investment	Support for strategy		Keep owners and bankers informed of plans and progress; seek buy-in	L	M
Industry associations (National Solid Waste Management Association)	Knowledge sharing	Knowledge sharing			L	M
Competitors (Allied Waste, Republic Services, Waste Management, regional companies)	Fair practices	Fair practices			L	M
Media (Waste and Recycling News, Trash Talk Today, Waste360.com, business journals)	Accountability	Objectivity; fair reporting			L	M

Stakeholder Network/Community

The next analysis looked at the current and potential relationships among WasteNot WantNot's stakeholders and identified ways to make them mutually beneficial. With a few exceptions, initial links among stakeholders were fairly weak, unknown or nonexistent; it fell to the company itself to draw key stakeholders with shared interests together into five distinct communities, each with a common purpose. In several instances, the company would need to seek out new stakeholders to join the community.

The five proposed groupings are depicted below:

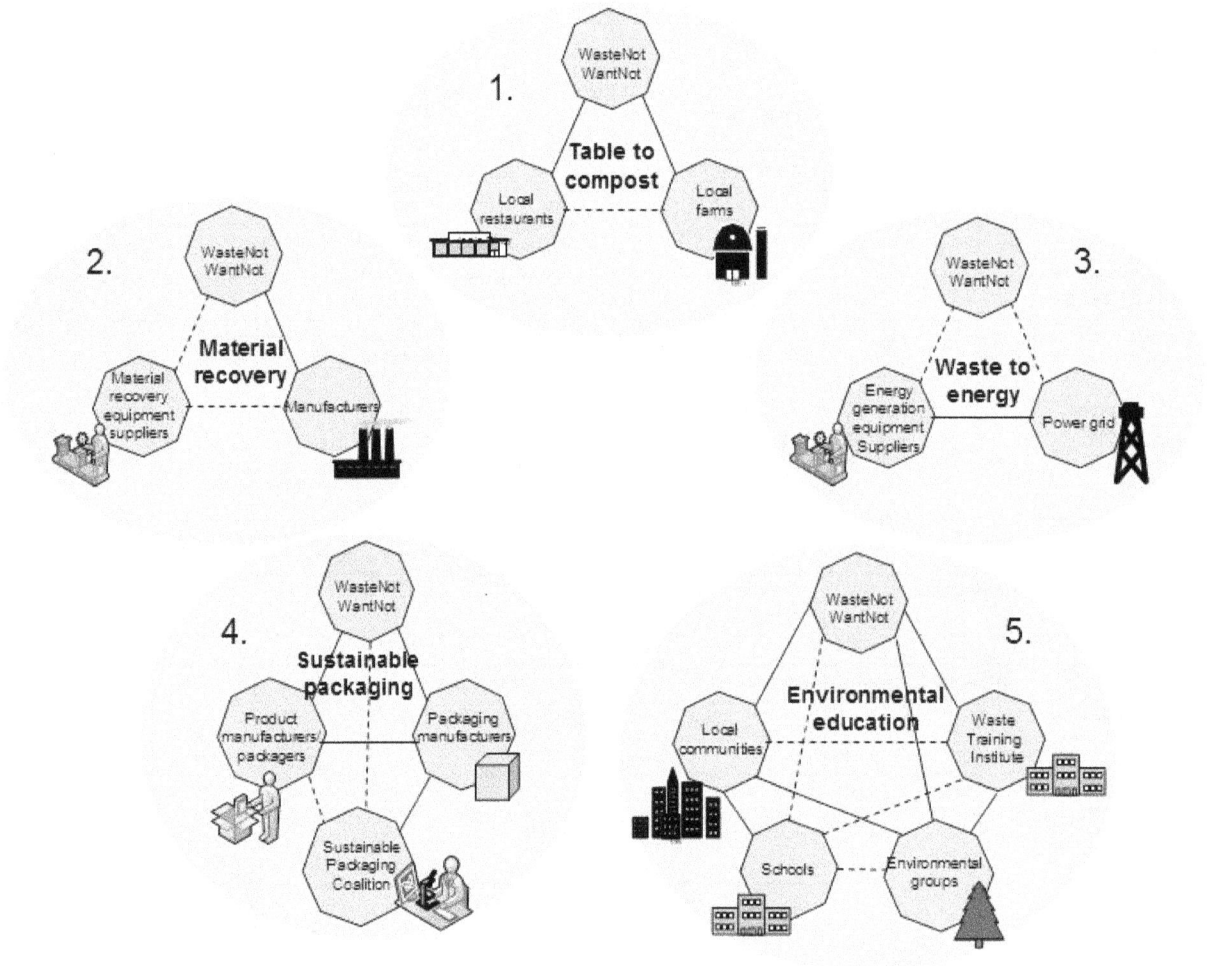

Group 1 links local restaurants, which generate significant amounts of compostable material, with local farms, who are likely users of the compost. WasteNot WantNot envisions establishing a composting facility and collecting kitchen and other compostable waste from restaurants, as well as households and other businesses, and converting the waste into usable compost for local farms. The company then intends to promote incorporation of local foods from those farms in restaurant menus, completing a virtuous cycle.

Group 2 seeks to partner WasteNot WantNot with suppliers and manufacturers to expand the amount of reusable material extracted from solid waste. The method for doing so, not yet determined, may range from more precise sorting to chemical processing that breaks down composite material into basic components. The company anticipates consulting with end users of recycled materials to identify their needs for raw materials, then researching to find the best opportunities and methods for recovering those materials.

Group 3 represents a brand new set of stakeholder relationships for WasteNot WantNot, who hopes to generate energy from waste for its own use and to resell any excess energy back to the power grid. Further investigation will be needed to select an optimal method from the range of choices that exist for generating energy from waste.

Group 4 comprises both existing and new manufacturing stakeholders, as well as an industry coalition with expertise in sustainable packaging. WasteNot WantNot hopes to reduce the amount of non-reusable packaging that ends up in its landfills and, as an added benefit, to reduce the environmental impact of whatever packaging remains.

Group 5 recognizes the need to educate the public about the impact of solid waste on the environment and to foster greater commitment to reduce, reuse and recycle waste products. It brings together the local communities and their schools with industry experts in waste management and other environmental groups.

Business Capital Inventory

WasteNot WantNot is privately owned and run by an experienced management team with a strong commitment to protecting the environment, providing a solid base of social and intellectual capital. The company is well capitalized and has a long history of solid financial management, ensuring an adequate reservoir of financial capital upon which to draw. The company owns and operates its own recycling facilities, landfills and a well-maintained fleet of collection vehicles, ensuring sufficient physical capital for current operations. However, several of the landfills are near capacity and will need to be replaced.

While corporate functions such as finance and research and development are centralized, operations are located and managed through a regional structure, enabling the company to reduce transportation costs and environmental impact while tailoring its services to the local market, and contributing to its organizational capital.

The company's market capital is solid, but has room for improvement. While the majority of its recycling operations are equipped to handle single stream processing, including most plastics, paper, glass and metal, its two oldest facilities require pre-sorting by customers and are limited in the types of materials they can accept. Currently none of the facilities is equipped for composting. Disposal of hazardous waste, including electronics, is subcontracted to a third party.

While the nature of its business provides significant environmental capital, the company has a sizeable carbon footprint that management would like to reduce. Because the existing fleet largely comprises diesel-fueled vehicles, and the operations rely on local utility companies for their energy needs, the company contributes significantly to greenhouse gas emissions.

Impact on WasteNot WantNot's social capital from stakeholders is mixed, although mostly positive. The company enjoys excellent relationships with the communities and businesses it serves, especially those where single stream recycling is in place. Communities served by the single stream process have on average 50% higher rates of recycling than those that do not. The company pays communities for recycling but charges for trash collection; hence, communities welcome single stream recycling as a means of reducing overall costs.

Although the company has received no overt complaints, the company would like to have closer relationships with communities where it operates. In several communities, its transfer stations account for a majority of the daily truck traffic in the area, sometimes causing congestion and considerable noise. Despite WasteNot WantNot's good track record in managing its landfills safely, residents and businesses in those communities remain apprehensive about the potential for leakages and odors from the landfill. Improving relationships with these communities would reduce the drain on the company's social capital.

Although its own drivers collect most of the solid waste processed by the company, it also accepts non-hazardous wastes from independent haulers. Those haulers who have access to the single stream processing are generally satisfied and easy to work with; those who must pre-sort the material are less satisfied and more difficult to work with, requiring considerable monitoring of deliveries to ensure properly sorted materials. Much of the documentation is paper-based, making it slow and prone to errors, creating a drain on the company's organizational capital.

The company holds all of the necessary licenses and permits for its operations, and its operations receive whatever public services are needed, ensuring adequate civic capital. It has knowledgeable partners in its supplier of the single stream sorting technology and among the users of the recycled materials.

Public support for recycling and other "green" initiatives is increasing, boosting WasteNot WantNot's visibility and image and, hence, its social capital. Due to the economic recession, WasteNot WantNot currently enjoys access to a strong labor market, helping to shore up its human capital.

Expanded SWOT Analysis

The company believes that it can improve its environmental effectiveness through investment in research and development in several areas, including increased material recovery and better packaging. Management also believes that the company can reduce its carbon footprint by upgrading its fleet and generating energy from solid wastes.

Much of the knowledge to make some of the improvements envisioned by management may come from third parties, including the company's suppliers and manufacturing customers, among others. New technology is constantly being developed to improve solid waste management techniques, increase material recovery and make packaging more sustainable. WasteNot WantNot hopes to tap into the knowledge base to adopt the best, leading edge technologies.

The company anticipates increasingly high standards for solid waste management in the future, including stricter air and water quality standards as well as more stringent requirements for landfills. It also expects to face greater competition for skilled labor as the economy picks up. While both of these developments are viewed as highly likely, neither is believed to present an overwhelming challenge.

Expanded SWOT Matrix

	Present +	Present −	Future +	Future −
Within Our Control	**Strength** Some single stream Commitment to sustainability	**Weakness** GHG emissions Some pre-sorting	**Potential** R&D breakthrough	**Risk** Landfills reach capacity
From Stakeholders	**Benefit** General goodwill Willingness to partner	**Detriment** Independent hauler annoyance Those near landfills	**Booster** Knowledge sharing	**Buster** Increasing standards for air/water quality, landfills
Beyond Our Control	**Advantage** Growing support for Environment Available labor pool	**Disadvantage** Remaining resistance	**Opportunity** New technologies	**Threat** Competition for labor

Mission, Values and Rules of Engagement

WasteNot WantNot reviewed and reaffirmed its mission as follows:

To mitigate the harmful effects of solid waste disposal on the environment and humanity by first reducing as much as possible the amount of waste generated and then maximizing the beneficial use and minimizing the negative effects of whatever remains. We do this wherever we are able, using the best technologies available, and we seek to continuously advance our knowledge and collaborate with others in developing and deploying new and better methods. To put it simply, "Waste nothing."

Upon review, WasteNot WantNot defined its most cherished values as: *Stewardship, Integrity, Transparency, Community*.

- *Stewardship:*   WasteNot WantNot believes that we are all stewards of the planet, and that we have an obligation to protect, replenish and preserve the earth's resources for current and future generations.

- *Integrity:*   The company strives to take a leadership role in promoting higher standards and in taking responsibility for their own shortcomings.

- *Transparency:*   The company freely shares its knowledge and insights, and provides information about its own performance to its stakeholders.

- *Community:*   WasteNot WantNot believes that their stakeholders are an integral part of their business, and they seek to engage them in open dialogue and mutual problem-solving.

WasteNot WantNot chose not to create specific written rules in support of their values. However, management has demonstrated commitment to these values through the company's policies, processes and actions. For instance, the company's headquarters and research center are LEED-silver certified, and preference is given to suppliers whose products are environmentally friendly. Employee meetings are held regularly to surface problems and solicit ideas, and a plan of action is established for those items selected by the employees. One such idea expanded and transformed the company's internal document shredding process to make it available as a service to businesses within their customer base. Progress is monitored and reported to company employees through newsletters and quarterly sessions, and stakeholders are frequently invited to participate on task forces and/or in review sessions.

Envisioning the Future

WasteNot WantNot's began this exercise with a vision linked directly to its mission and articulated as follows:

WasteNot WantNot has made solid waste reduction, reuse, recycling and recovery a win-win opportunity for everyone.

To help guide the process, they established the following guiding principles:

- *Make it easy and cost-effective to do the right thing (i.e., reduce, reuse, recycle, recover)*

- *Protect human and other habitats from harm, including air pollution, greenhouse gas emissions, and water and soil contamination.*

- *Enable everyone to share in the benefits of environmental stewardship.*

WasteNot WantNot chose the year 2020 as the time horizon for achieving their vision. Next, working in small teams, the company developed visions of the future for various stakeholders, as summarized below.

A. **Communities, businesses and construction companies** *recycle as much solid waste as possible because we have made it cheaper and easier to do so than any other disposal option.*

- *It is cheaper because they are reimbursed for recycling but must pay for trash collection.*

- *It is easier because we offer single stream recycling, accept all types of materials, and provide composting of kitchen and yard waste.*

B. **Manufacturers** *use less packaging overall and the packaging they use is easily reused or recycled. They partner with us to design better packaging alternatives that meet their functional needs while protecting the environment.*

C. **Suppliers** *partner with us to continuously improve the efficiency and environmental effectiveness of our processes, including solid waste collection, single stream recycling, composting, material recovery, energy from waste and landfill transformation.*

D. **Manufacturers and farms** *use as much recycled or recovered as possible in lieu of virgin materials because we have made it easy and cost-effective to do so.*

- *Materials are recovered, sorted and bundled to their specifications, making it ready to use (or as close as possible) as input to their manufacturing processes*

E. **Local communities** *where we operate welcome us as a strategic partner in making their communities safe, enjoyable places to live and work.*

- *We engage them regularly in dialogue and partner with them in initiatives that affect them.*

- *We ensure quiet out-of-the-way operations, avoiding traffic congestion and other disruptions.*

- *We are proactive in preventing odors, leaks and air, water, or soil contamination at landfills and compost heaps.*

- *We partner with them to transform closed landfills into safe, attractive community parks and recreation areas, or other public uses.*

F. ***Employees, investors, regulators*** *and all of our other stakeholders love us because our environmental leadership has made us a sustainable business throughout the economic business cycle.*

- *We provide steady economic growth and job security in our communities.*

- *We operate efficiently and safely and provide environmental leadership and education.*

- *We consistently engage our stakeholders in open dialogue and seek their feedback.*

Strategy Mapping

Outcome perspective

WasteNot WantNot began their strategy map with their mission, values and vision (which they dubbed their "20/20 Vision").

Stakeholder perspective

The company translated the vision into the following objectives and goals:
:

- *Reduce the generation of solid waste per household or business site within the communities we serve by 20% by the year 2020.*

- *Increase the reused/recycled proportion of non-hazardous materials we collect by 20% by the year 2020.*

- *Increase the number of households and businesses served by 20% by the year 2020.*

- *Reduce our GHG emissions by 20% by the year 2020.*

- *Reduce our reliance on non-renewable energy by 20% by the year 2020.*

In addition, they agreed on two broad qualitative objectives:

- *Address the specific needs and concerns of stakeholders, including material users, employees, communities and the general public.*

- *Ensure a fair return on investment to our investors.*

WasteNot WantNot's value propositions and exchanges formed the basis of their strategies:

- *Identify and promote alternatives that reduce packaging waste.*

- *Promote single-stream recycling to encourage participation.*

- *Develop and implement material recovery techniques.*

- *Upgrade our fleet to hybrid or electric engines.*

- *Use methane from our landfills for power generation.*

- *Promote our services within communities and businesses in close proximity to existing customers.*

- *Transform our landfills to parkland or other public use.*

- *Provide job security/ employee development opportunities.*

- *Provide recycled materials in user-ready form.*

- *Provide educational programs and materials for the general public regarding waste management practices as it impacts them and their communities.*

- *Engage stakeholders in each of these initiatives to gain insights and earn their support.*

Process perspective

To achieve the objectives they have chosen, the company identified the crucial processes that together create value for their stakeholders and build their business capital.

- *Establish research teams to investigate packaging and material recovery possibilities.*

- *Develop partnerships with key product manufacturers and end users of recycled materials.*

- *Develop stakeholder feedback processes.*

- *Promote our services to adjacent communities.*

- *Implement waste to power generation, landfill transformation, GHG emission reduction and public education.*

- *Design employee involvement program.*

- *Evaluate and prioritize all major initiatives using cost/benefit analyses and business cases.*

Resources and Capabilities perspective

The company identified critical success factors, such as stakeholder buy-in, an educated research staff, proper laboratory and processing equipment, adequate funding, excellent relationship management practices, and approvals and licenses. From there, they developed the following resource and capability objectives:

- *Communicate intent to stakeholders.*

- *Recruit and train R&D experts and stakeholder relationship managers.*

- *Organize research library and laboratory.*

- *Establish budget for new initiatives.*

- *Align performance goals and incentives; reward innovation.*

- *Upgrade fleet; acquire equipment for power generation and land transformation.*

- *Measure and monitor GHG emissions.*

- *Obtain approvals and licenses.*

The resulting strategy map is shown on the following page.

Sample "Waste Not, Want Not" Strategy Map

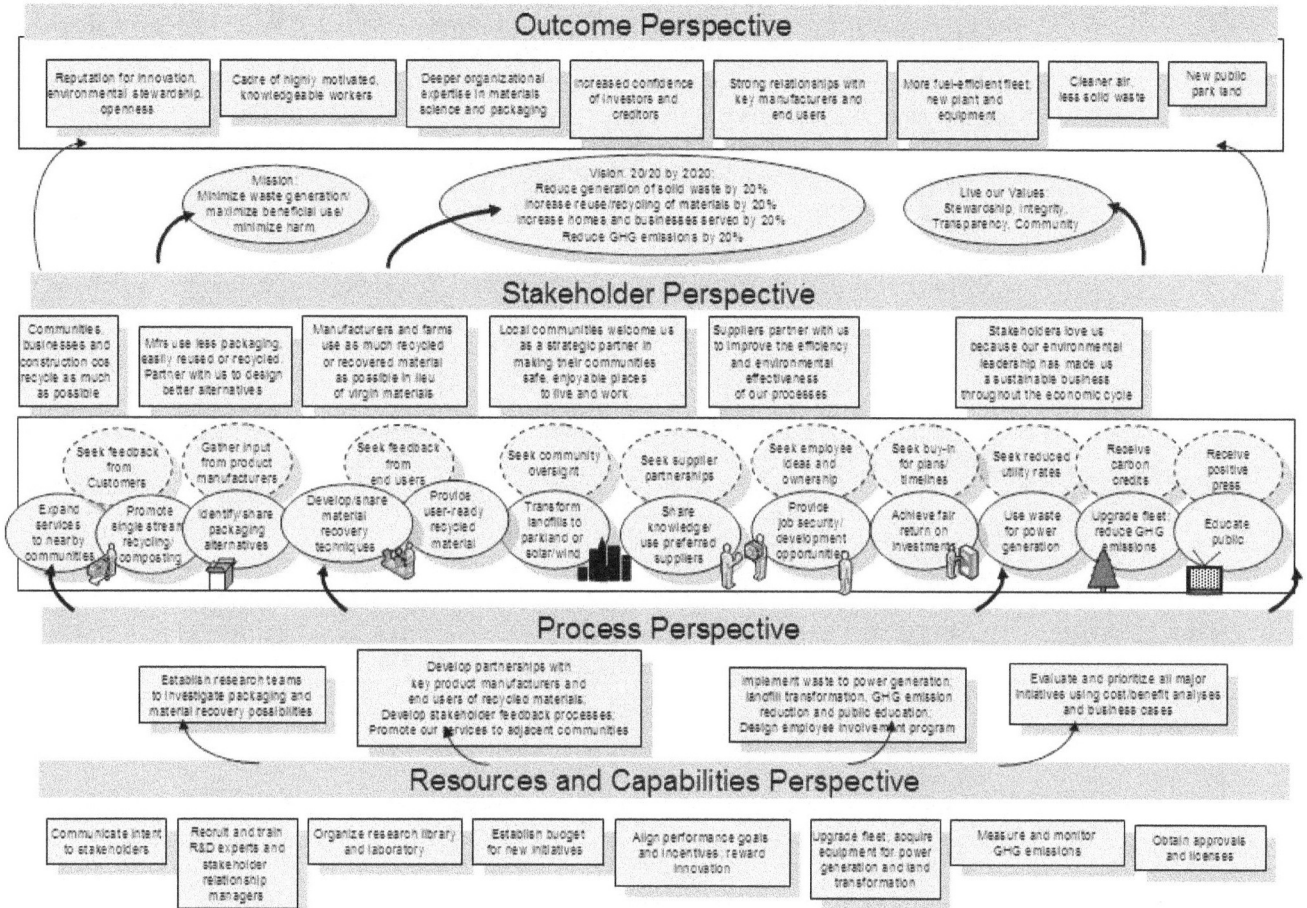

Outcome Perspective

| Reputation for innovation, environmental stewardship, openness | Cadre of highly motivated, knowledgeable workers | Deeper organizational expertise in materials science and packaging | Increased confidence of investors and creditors | Strong relationships with key manufacturers and end users | More fuel-efficient fleet; new plant and equipment | Cleaner air, less solid waste | New public park land |

Mission:
Minimize waste generation/
maximize beneficial use/
minimize harm

Vision: 20/20 by 2020:
Reduce generation of solid waste by 20%
Increase reuse/recycling of materials by 20%
Increase homes and businesses served by 20%
Reduce GHG emissions by 20%

Live our Values:
Stewardship, Integrity,
Transparency, Community

Stakeholder Perspective

| Communities, businesses and construction cos recycle as much as possible | Mfrs use less packaging, easily reused or recycled. Partner with us to design better alternatives | Manufacturers and farms use as much recycled or recovered material as possible in lieu of virgin materials | Local communities welcome us as a strategic partner in making their communities safe, enjoyable places to live and work | Suppliers partner with us to improve the efficiency and environmental effectiveness of our processes | Stakeholders love us because our environmental leadership has made us a sustainable business throughout the economic cycle |

Seek feedback from Customers — Gather input from product manufacturers — Seek feedback from end users — Seek community oversight — Seek supplier partnerships — Seek employee ideas and ownership — Seek buy-in for plans/ timelines — Seek reduced utility rates — Receive carbon credits — Receive positive press

Expand services to nearby communities — Promote single stream recycling/ composting — Identify/share packaging alternatives — Develop/share material recovery techniques — Provide user-ready recycled material — Transform landfills to parkland or solar/wind — Share knowledge/ use preferred suppliers — Provide job security/ development opportunities — Achieve fair return on investment — Use waste for power generation — Upgrade fleet; reduce GHG emissions — Educate public

Process Perspective

| Establish research teams to investigate packaging and material recovery possibilities | Develop partnerships with key product manufacturers and end users of recycled materials; Develop stakeholder feedback processes; Promote our services to adjacent communities | Implement waste to power generation; landfill transformation, GHG emission reduction and public education; Design employee involvement program | Evaluate and prioritize all major initiatives using cost/benefit analyses and business cases |

Resources and Capabilities Perspective

| Communicate intent to stakeholders | Recruit and train R&D experts and stakeholder relationship managers | Organize research library and laboratory | Establish budget for new initiatives | Align performance goals and incentives; reward innovation | Upgrade fleet; acquire equipment for power generation and land transformation | Measure and monitor GHG emissions | Obtain approvals and licenses |

Adapted from Strategy Maps, *Robert S. Kaplan & David P. Norton, Harvard Business School Press, 2004*

Strategic Scorecard

Among the outcomes to be achieved were such measures as the reduction in non-recyclable solid waste per household, the increase in households served, the reduction in greenhouse gas emissions and the company's return on investment. Performance drivers to support those outcomes included such measures as the number of improvement ideas generated, the creation of outreach plans, the establishment of the baseline for greenhouse gas emissions, and the implementation of a company-wide structured process for planning and evaluating proposed initiatives.

Once the outcomes and performance drivers were identified, the company established specific target values for each, both short run and long run. The strategy was informally dubbed the company's "20/20 Vision" in acknowledgement of both the key targets and the time horizon. The label quickly became the accepted name company-wide for the overall strategy.

Below is a snapshot of the company's strategic scorecard. Due to limited readability, only the long term goals are shown.

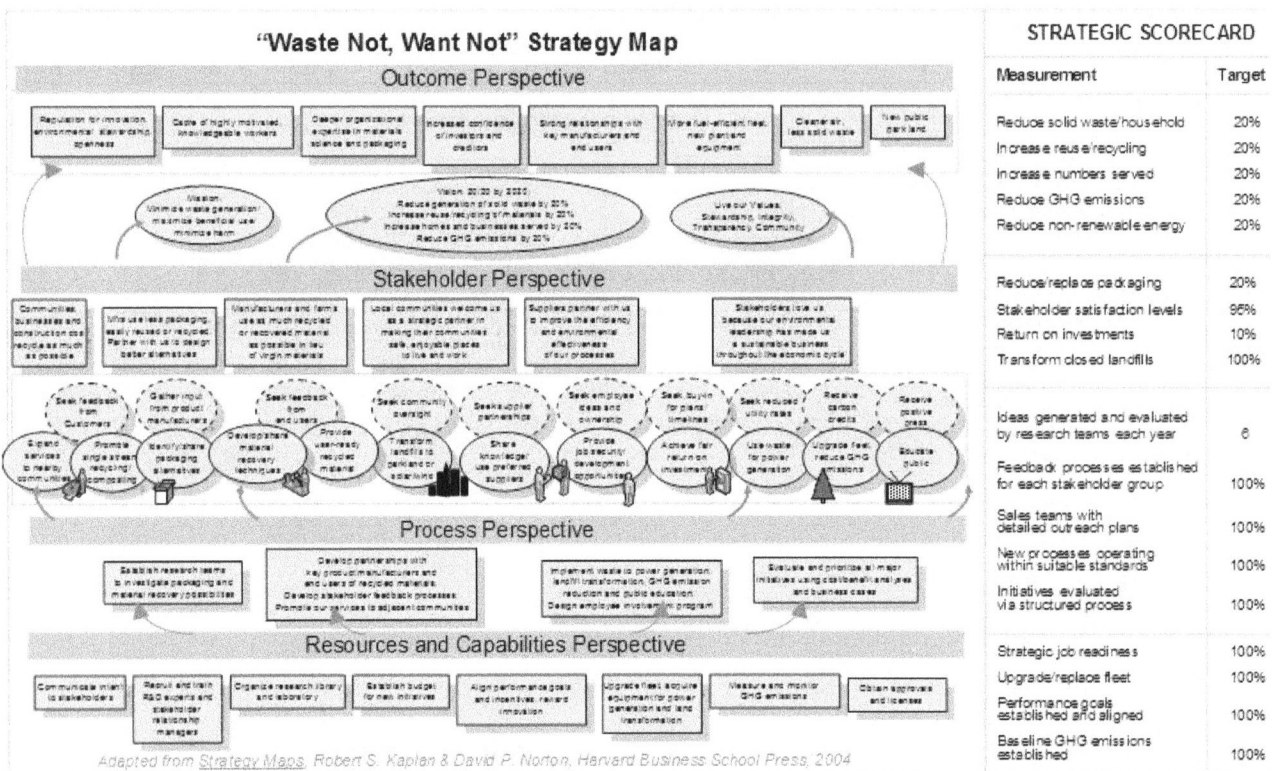

"Waste Not, Want Not" Strategy Map

Adapted from Strategy Maps, Robert S. Kaplan & David P. Norton, Harvard Business School Press, 2004

STRATEGIC SCORECARD

Measurement	Target
Reduce solid waste/household	20%
Increase reuse/recycling	20%
Increase numbers served	20%
Reduce GHG emissions	20%
Reduce non-renewable energy	20%
Reduce/replace packaging	20%
Stakeholder satisfaction levels	95%
Return on investments	10%
Transform closed landfills	100%
Ideas generated and evaluated by research teams each year	6
Feedback processes established for each stakeholder group	100%
Sales teams with detailed outreach plans	100%
New processes operating within suitable standards	100%
Initiatives evaluated via structured process	100%
Strategic job readiness	100%
Upgrade/replace fleet	100%
Performance goals established and aligned	100%
Baseline GHG emissions established	100%

Project Prioritization

Upon reviewing their strategy and conducting cost/benefit analyses, WasteNot WantNot quickly identified a small number of initiatives—the "no-brainers" —where the costs were manageable and the benefits were potentially significant. These included upgrading the remaining operations to single stream processing, establishing a composting operation in partnership with local farms and restaurants, and upgrading the fleet to hybrid or electric engines. In addition, they green-lit community and stakeholder outreach and educational initiatives, including investigation of the detailed needs of manufacturers using their materials as feedstock. Use of mobile technology for independent haulers was approved for further study, with implementation to be deferred until a final business case could be made.

Management recognized that significant challenges lay ahead for several initiatives which, although their impact was projected to be extremely high, placed extraordinary demand on the organization's resources and required significant acquisition of talent and infrastructure. These initiatives included transformation of closed landfills, energy generation from waste, improved material recovery and reductions in packaging. After further analysis, it was determined that the first two projects should be given top priority, and that the latter two would be researched but no action taken until a later date.

Project teams were established for each of the approved initiatives, while WasteNot WantNot's management provides ongoing oversight to the strategic portfolio. Progress reports are prepared monthly, while in-depth reviews are conducted quarterly on the most crucial projects. Funding for capital improvements is released in phases, based on the satisfactory progress of the respective initiative. Change requests may be submitted at any time.

Strategic Alignment

Each WasteNot WantNot project team was charged with the responsibility of assessing the impact of the initiative on the organization and making recommendations to ensure internal alignment of people, processes and systems. For the "no-brainer" projects, this was fairly straightforward.

- The upgrading of operations would adopt the structure and best practices already in use elsewhere within the company, restructuring roles and responsibilities of existing personnel and providing appropriate training in single stream operations. Sales representatives would receive guidance in negotiating new agreements with customers in the affected areas.

- Upgrading of the fleet required few adjustments other than training for drivers, routers and mechanics.

- Establishing a composting operation was an entirely new line of business, requiring new processes, equipment, systems, and roles and responsibilities, adopted from similar operations at other companies. The new positions would be filled through a combination of external hires of experienced personnel and retraining of qualified internal candidates.

- The stakeholder outreach and community education initiatives required some training for customer contact personnel and environmental project managers, as well as creation of a cadre of skilled presenters. Some adjustments to compensation were proposed to reflect the increased responsibilities and requisite skill level.

The remaining initiatives were largely investigative in nature, hence little re-alignment was needed in the initial stage other than defining roles and responsibilities for the members of the task force, along with some variable compensation for their added responsibilities. Consideration was given to adjusting the compensation of their colleagues as well, since they might be shouldering more of the day-to-day work; a small bonus pool was established to be used on a case-by-case basis.

Once each team had developed its own internal alignment plan, the management team reviewed them together to ensure consistency across the organization. The human resources department, working closely with Finance, reviewed all new positions to ensure a compensation structure commensurate with responsibility. Posting of new positions was coordinated to ensure that employees had a complete picture of the potential opportunities before deciding which ones to pursue.

Alignment work will continue throughout the strategic planning time horizon, especially as the more complex initiatives move beyond the study phase into implementation.

Organizational Change/Transformation

Early on, project teams were brought together with company leadership to share the overall strategic vision of the company and to present how each initiative fit into the design. The strategic scorecard was reviewed and considerable time was devoted to raising and addressing questions. Some excellent ideas were surfaced and incorporated into the relevant projects, while open issues were assigned to senior managers for further analysis and follow up. A reconnect session was scheduled for six weeks later.

Managers conducted individual work sessions with their units, some in person, some by phone or video conference, and others by webcast. A video of the previous leadership session was included, along with various online materials outlining the mission, vision and strategy and the initiatives being undertaken. An internal blog site was established, along with several other communication methods, to enable employees to raise questions, share concerns and offer ideas.

An employee survey was conducted following the rollout of the strategy, with a response rate of 53%. All employees received a letter signed by the chief executive inviting them to participate in the survey. In addition to paper-based and on-line surveys, employees in remote sites were given a further option of participating in an on-site session led by an outside facilitator.

Although some questioned the relevance to their own lives, the response was generally favorable. The strongest resistance came from workers in the oldest operations, where the shift to single stream recycling was seen as making their jobs more difficult and where some workers were worried that they were being replaced. In response, senior management spent time on site through multiple visits, meeting with employees, providing reassurances and addressing their concerns. Through a combination of teambuilding, training and incentive programs, the issues were resolved and the oldest site volunteered to become the pilot for the composting operation as well.

Cascading Goals and Objectives

Through the manager-led work sessions and project team meetings, employees learned about the company's strategic scorecard and discussed how their work would contribute toward the goals. Where appropriate, work team and individual goals and milestones were established in support of the company goals. While many of the goals were primarily the responsibility of the project teams, everyone was expected to provide support to those teams as well as ensuring that their own processes were operating effectively and that they and their units acquired and maintained the appropriate skill sets through training and coaching.

Progress toward the company goals and milestones is reported monthly to management, and published and disseminated to all employees every quarter. Results are color-coded based on the current status—green for "on track", yellow for "at risk", and red for "in trouble - needs action now." For instance, initial discussions regarding transformation of one of the landfills nearing capacity broke down when a key local public official was caught up in an unrelated bribery scandal that had the community in an uproar. That initiative is currently operating under a yellow code until such time as the official is exonerated or replaced.

Although it is too early to tell whether the company will be successful in achieving its vision, people are feeling good about the impact their company expects to have on the environment and are excited to be a part of making it happen, hence their human capital is at its peak. As their story gets out, their social capital will undoubtedly increase as well, providing additional momentum toward achieving their goals.

Conclusion

Chances are, if you have made it this far, you were already a believer in the underlying premise that taking care of the legitimate needs of all of your stakeholders offers you the best chance for long term success. If not, perhaps we have helped you see the world a little bit differently. In any case, we hope that you have found some useful ideas and techniques that you can take with you to your next planning session. Your thoughts and feedback are welcome. Please join us through our website (www.queensbridgeconsultancy.com).